W9-CNR-723

What the Experts Are Saying About Joe Marconi on Marketing

This is a remarkable book in that someone has finally explored the important role that the concept of experience plays in marketing. Why hasn't anyone explained this before? If you're in any part of the marketing industry, you should *experience* this book.

> Joe Cappo, author of *"The Future of Advertising: New Media, New Clients, New Consumers in the Post-Television Age"* and former publisher of *Advertising Age* about **Creating the Marketing Experience**

Advances in technology, education, and consumer sophistication have changed both the rules and the expectations for marketers in the twenty-first century. In **Creating the Marketing Experience,** Joe Marconi looks at the trends, challenges, and opportunities that define the marketing landscape of today and tomorrow. This book offers intelligent and creative strategies for building solid business relationships.

Gary Slack
Chairman & Chief Experience Officer
Slack Barshinger

Informative, spin-free, and right on target. Required reading for anyone who wants to design and implement a winning program.

Tom Asacker, author of *Sandbox Wisdom: Revolutionize Your Brand with the Genius of Childhood* about **Public Relations: The Complete Guide**

His comprehensive insights serve as invaluable information . . . and timely reminders to the seasoned professional.

Terry J. Erdmann, Motion Picture Publicist, author of *Star Trek: The Deep Space Nine Companion* about **Public Relations: The Complete Guide**

. . . When I see Joe Marconi's name on a finished book, it's different. I tend to look into that one, else I might be missing something.

James Brady, Editor-at-Large, *Advertising Age* about **The Brand Marketing Book**

People in business are faced with creating a marketing vision for tomorrow. Joe Marconi . . . is an insightful prophet of trends and future Marketing.

Viki King, Author of *How to Write a Movie in 21 Days: The Inner Movie Method* about **Future Marketing**

Creating the Marketing Experience

Creating the Marketing Experience

New Strategies for Building Relationships with Your Target Market

JOE MARCONI

RACOM
COMMUNICATIONS

THOMSON

Australia · Brazil · Canada · Mexico · Singapore · Spain · United Kingdom · United States

THOMSON

━━━━━✦━━━━━ ™

Creating the Marketing Experience: New Strategies for Building Relationships with Your Target Market
Joe Marconi

COPYRIGHT © 2005 by Texere, an imprint of Thomson/South-Western, a part of The Thomson Corporation. Thomson and the Star logo are trademarks used herein under license.

Consulting Editor in Marketing: Richard Hagle

Composed by: Sans Serif Inc.

Printed in the United States of America by RR Donnelley Crawfordsville, IN

1 2 3 4 5 08 07 06 05
This book is printed on acid-free paper.

ISBN: 0-324-20544-9

This publication is designed to provide accurate and authoritative information in regard to the subject matter covered. It is sold with the understanding that the publisher is not engaged in rendering legal, accounting, or other professional services. If expert assistance is required, the services of a competent professional person should be sought.

ALL RIGHTS RESERVED.
No part of this work covered by the copyright hereon may be reproduced or used in any form or by any means—graphic, electronic, or mechanical, including photocopying, recording, taping, Web distribution, or information storage and retrieval systems, or in any other manner—without the written permission of the publisher.

The names of all companies or products mentioned herein are used for identification purposes only and may be trademarks or registered trademarks of their respective owners. Texere disclaims any affiliation, association, connection with, sponsorship, or endorsements by such owners.

For permission to use material from this text or product, submit a request online at http://www.thomsonrights.com.

Library of Congress Cataloging in Publication Number is available. See page 336 for details.

For more information about our products, contact us at:

Thomson Learning Academic Resource Center
1-800-423-0563

Thomson Higher Education
5191 Natorp Boulevard
Mason, Ohio 45040
USA

For Todd and Kristin and Emily
And for Karin

CONTENTS

───────

Introduction

Experience is *actual*. It is not information acquired simply by the authority of others, who themselves may or may not have learned from experience. The experience can be subtle or explosive, but when effective it can determine whether people become merely *aware* of something or if they choose to make it a part of their lives.

A positive experience can create a strong

connection between a person and a subject. Such connections can be memorable and long lasting, prompting not only an initial response, such as a purchase
decision or other type of commitment, but can potentially evolve into feelings of loyalty to a brand or a
cause. This fact is extremely important to those of us
engaged in marketing, where creating connections and
relationships is often a major, if not primary, objective
of our efforts.

What constitutes a "marketing experience"? Is an
experience only interactive? Does it require physical
participation between a consumer and the subject?
Can laughing, crying, cheering, or some other verbal
response be considered an experience? Test-driving a
car is an experience, but can a daydream or fantasy in
which someone imagines the thrill, pleasure, comfort,
pride, or exhilaration of driving a car be an
experience?

Consider the amusement park ride that propels a
person to great heights, turns sharply, then plummets
at breathtakingly high speed, and repeats the process
several times in a short period. Exiting the ride, the
person pauses for a moment to regain a sense of balance and equilibrium.

Now imagine a person at a theme park climbing
aboard one of the virtual thrill rides, such as the "Star
Tours" ride at Disney World or the "Back to the Future" ride at Universal Studios. Both rides use combi-

nations of sensory imagery—film, sound, mirror-effects, and a motorized chair—to create the illusion or sensation of propelling a person to great heights, turning sharply, then plummeting at what seems to be breathtakingly high speed, and repeats the process several times in a short period—all while the person and the "ride" remain in place.

Which person walks away feeling as if he or she just had an exciting, heart-racing experience? Of course the answer is *they both did.* One was real, while the other created the illusion of being real, but basically, "they did it with mirrors."

A marketing experience can be intensely physical or strongly emotional, but the one that qualifies as the *true* marketing experience is the one that works. The goal is to achieve the objective, not to argue about the definitions of the processes. Creating the marketing experience is the process of developing a connection that links the product, the brand, the company, a person, or an issue that is the subject of a marketing effort. The most effective marketing programs engage the consumer and create a connection or a presence, often without people even realizing that is what is happening.

In the mid-1950s, the psychologist Dr. Abraham Maslow[1] developed the theory he termed the *hierarchy of needs.* It examined both the physiological needs of humans, such as for air, food, and water, and the emotional needs, such as for safety, security, esteem, and the need to belong. Years later, marketers would create ways and means to tap into these needs to attract attention and influence decisions. Consider how much dining at the hottest restaurant in town or wearing the latest designer label promotes a sense of acceptance or makes a public statement about one's having achieved a level of success or status.

While the essential marketing processes haven't changed much through the years, what *have* changed are the public's expectations of marketers and other service providers. Education, technology, and personal wealth have all evolved to the point where people don't just satisfy their needs by doing or getting what they want, but they expect the providers of what they want to be constantly working to make the process better, more efficient, and meaningful on a number of levels.

Professor Bernd H. Schmitt of Columbia University, in discussing *experiential marketing*—a process that encourages customers to sense, feel, think, act, and relate to a subject—has concluded that, "More and more marketers are moving away from traditional 'features and benefits' marketing toward creating experiences for their customers."[2]

Yet, weren't we marketers *supposed* to be creating such experiences all along? Getting away from "features and benefits" marketing—which explains, then reinforces, to consumers why they initially choose, then *continue* to choose the particular brands they do—is usually a first step to removing the underpinnings of consumer satisfaction and loyalty, the qualities that define the relationship between the company, organization, or brand and its constituency.

Whether to develop a program around features and benefits or around sensory experiences does not have to be an either/or proposition. Why not do *both*? To focus on the sensing, feeling, and relating components while de-emphasizing features and benefits is, *selling the sizzle and not the steak.* Even in the most health-conscious of times, people quickly become hungry again and remember a plate full of sizzle is not enough to satisfy their appetites. It is probably true that while getting customers to sense, feel, think, act, and relate to a subject has indeed always been part of the job for marketers, some of us have forgotten it from time to time or, alas, have simply done a poor job of it.

Sergio Zyman, formerly the chief marketing officer of the Coca-Cola Company, raised more than a few eyebrows in the profession when he announced with a great flourish that, " . . . The era of marketing as we have known it is over, dead, kaput—and most marketers don't realize it."[3]

Rather interestingly, Mr. Zyman then added, "I love marketing. I know it can work when it's done right. And it's beautiful when it does. The problem with marketing today is that for the past twenty or thirty years, marketers have been caught up in the trappings of marketing . . . and have forgotten that their job is to sell stuff."

So it's not so much *marketing* that's "over, dead, kaput"—it's only *bad* marketing, as perhaps practiced by people who've taken their eyes off the ball, so to speak, and lost the true focus of what they were supposed to be doing, that is now, in Mr. Zyman's opinion, uh, deceased.

Based on this interpretation, it could also be stated emphatically that making movies, television programs and music, providing banking services, delivering packages, and cutting hair are also dead because a number of people today take good money for doing what they do so badly. Is it the process that's failed or the people managing and implementing the process that have failed?

Being innovative in creating relationships with the consumer public or another designated target group is not enough by itself to build loyalty or to sustain those relationships. Consumers tune out many of the most creative sales pitches, convinced that they have seen it all, heard it all, and, in the vast ocean of clutter, they choose to ignore our aggressive and well-intentioned attempts at brand differentiation.

We marketers and managers are on a seemingly never-ending quest to discover the "Next Big

Thing"—whatever will be the big breakthrough trend or flavor-of-the month regardless of the industry, product, or subject category. What we *really* want and often need are new or different applications to more effectively market whatever we have—new products, old brands, events, theme parks, issues, causes, features, personalities, or places.

Creating the Marketing Experience provides a guide for marketing professionals and managers through a range of strategies that include—and at times go beyond—traditional advertising, public relations, and direct marketing approaches in order to build and maintain deeper, more personal relationships, grow market share, enhance brand equity, and increase public awareness and customer loyalty.

The *experience* may be the result of one idea or a mix of tactical or interactive systems and media. It might include art, entertainment, an event, or one or more personalized pleasures, such as product sampling or testing, wine tasting, a "bake-off," or a festival with a creative mix of elements that create a connection between the consumer and the company, organization, and the brand.

This is a book for marketing professionals, advertising and public relations practitioners, managers, entrepreneurs, fundraisers, recruiters, and, not so coincidentally, for CEOs and directors who have the ultimate responsibility for bringing and holding the program, company, or business together. It is a book about doing it all. And making it an experience.

For their assistance in making this book an experience, special thanks to my editor and friend Rich Hagle; to Joe Cappo, Lonny Bernardi, Rich Girod, and Guy Kendler; to Paula Block and Pam Newton of Viacom and Paramount Studios; and to Karin Gottschalk Marconi for her continued help and support.

Notes

1. Biographical references to Dr. Abraham Maslow (1908–1970) by Dr. C. George Boeree. Psychology Department, Shippensburg University, Personality Theories online at www.ship.edu/~cgboeree/maslow.html.
2. Quotation from "Experiential Marketing" by Bernd H. Schmitt (New York: The Free Press, 1999).
3. Quotation attributed to Sergio Zyman first appeared in the book *The End of Marketing As We Know It* by Sergio Zyman. New York: HarperCollins, 1999.

Planning the Marketing Experience

Introduction to Part One

Creating the Marketing Experience is in two sections. Part One is the section that explains what we are doing, why we are doing it, and how it works. From a logical starting point of first *understanding* the marketing experience, through the role research plays in each step of the process, to crafting the plan and setting it in motion, this section creates a context to better understand what follows. And what follows is a series of case studies detailing practical applications of the marketing experience in actual practice.

In a time of rapid change, it is reasonable to assume that *some* things will remain the same—basic definitions of terms we know and use. Alas, just as ethics is now viewed as being not so much a matter of right or wrong, it is reinterpreted to apply to particular situation, as in "The action is wrong . . . but, under certain mitigating circumstances, it is not *always* wrong."

The Marketing Experience takes what we know of the practice of marketing and activates our efforts in a somehow unique way—to have it stand apart from traditional marketing programs. What constitutes this activation process is the subject of some debate. Must an experience be interactive? Does creating a mood that emotionally touches someone qualify as *experiential*? It is surprising how some people can be so rigid in defining or interpreting terms. This is less a book about terms and more about getting the job done.

Understanding the Marketing Experience

Marketing is a process that operates on many levels. When managed correctly, it is constantly evolving, reflecting the needs, desires, and changes in the marketplace. The *most* effective marketing programs are those that create a presence and achieve their objectives without the consumers who are the targets of the effort even being aware that is what's happening.

Such achievements are not realized through trickery, but rather by a process of putting the brand, product, issue, or subject into consumers' lives and consciousness, and creating a bond. After a while consumers no longer notice that the brand's logo has become so much a fixed part of their surroundings . . . but they always know it's there.

Programming a TiVo system to record a favorite television program; maintaining a schedule, calendar, or screen saver on a laptop, notebook, or hand-held computer; choosing a favorite photo scene or theme to be depicted on a Visa or MasterCard—a theme that reflects the cardholder's personal tastes or interests, from sailing to Scrabble to Impressionist art—are only a few of the methods smart marketers employ to seamlessly integrate a logo or message on a branded product with subtlety into consumers' lives.

Good marketing becomes invisibly interwoven into the lifestyles of the people in the targeted markets.

A new home, for example, offers features that provide joy and comfort, such as a spectacular view, a swimming pool, an exercise room, or access to golf or tennis. Each of these features—sometimes labeled and branded, sometimes not—creates an *experience* that actively and physically involves and connects the person to the home in such a way as to reinforce the message or value statement that initially sealed the deal.

This makes the original decision to buy or rent an active and personal one as the consumer continues to be reminded of the decision and connection through repeated use. The comfort features become, in short, part of the *marketing experiences* that invite the person's attention, help close the deal, and keep the customer satisfied.

What? Isn't it a stretch to suggest an ocean view or a garden could be a marketing message? It's no more of a stretch than a Buick symbol or a BMW logo on a car key being a continuing reinforcement of a purchase decision long after the imprint has ceased to be consciously noticed. Familiar articles and surroundings that are parts of life's routine experiences unconsciously bind the subject to the consumer.

While an effective marketing experience is generally a good deal more interactive and physical, sometimes a powerful *emotional* or *sensory experience* can be stirring enough to create a connection between a company and a consumer, a seller and a buyer.

The marketer's goal is mostly and ultimately about making the sale and getting the business. But the marketing process is also about connecting with a defined segment of the public and turning that connection into some type of relationship—whether the focus is on creating awareness of a product, a service, or brand; selling something; promoting an idea; changing a perception; encouraging an endorsement or referral; or doing whatever is most appropriate to generate the desired response.

Marketing encompasses *packaging, positioning, pricing, promotion, distribution,* and *sales.* Advertising and public relations typically fall under the promotion budget, though PR is certainly every bit as informational and educational as it is promotional, a point that causes some public relations practitioners to bristle a bit when they suspect their professional credibility is being threatened, diminished, or limited by their work being placed under the marketing umbrella.

For purposes of this work, however, PR will be regarded as not only a part but in most cases, *a very pivotal part* of the marketing mix.

The term "marketing" itself has numerous definitions from the very simple and concise to the very rambling-though-scholarly, and practitioners have freely chosen to accept the size that suits their purposes.

A prominent authority on marketing describes it as "the process in which decisions are made in a totally interrelated changing business environment on all the activities that facilitate change in order that the targeted group of customers are satisfied and the defined objectives are accomplished."[1] The American Marketing Association regards marketing as "the performance of business to consumer or user."[2] It's the same idea seen from different angles and interpreted by different practitioners.

For years marketing was considered to be about the presentation of products and services in ways that led to the completion of the sale. Increasingly, however, marketing principles evolved that helped consumers determine how they felt about the products and services. While sales and profits are certainly what business is about, in some instances marketing campaigns are set in motion without the sale being the primary objective. Creating or changing public opinion is sometimes the goal itself.

People who never even owned or used a particular product or tried a service themselves might still recommend it to others based on the favorable opinions they have of how individuals, organizations, or companies present their messages. It is not unusual to hear someone say "That's a good company," without actually having any personal experience with the company, but because he or she respects its (or its executives') public stand on a particular social issue.

For example, people who did not own cars—thus had no use for gasoline—might still hold and share the opinion that Mobil Oil is a good company because for years it has awarded significant financial grants to the

Public Broadcasting System, making possible the cultural programming of television shows, most notably *Masterpiece Theater*. Or that the Ford Motor Company is a good company because it created the Ford Foundation, which in turn funds programs that help people. Many segments of the public enthusiastically praise and admire companies and organizations that support the arts, women's rights, spiritual programs and issues, gay rights, ethnic pride, and any number of other special interests.

Ultimately, marketing principles have been adapted and applied to areas other than products. The subject of a marketing effort can be a cause, issue, intellectual property, or people, from entertainers, athletes, doctors, and authors to chefs, politicians, statesmen, and corporate executives.

In today's environment a fire fighter, pilot, or high school student might achieve some level of notoriety and become the subject of a book, a film, an event, media and lecture tours, a comic book, plastic action figure, or all of the above and, as such, may be the central focus of a broad-reaching marketing program. On a less dramatic level, the choice of a dentist or a family lawyer might be made as the result of a marketing effort, such as sponsorship or other identification with a community group or organization.

The best marketing efforts are often seamlessly woven into the consumer's routine and consciousness.

Consider the local insurance agents who for decades have donated free book covers and calendars displaying their names and logos to local schools, or savings institutions that distribute plastic piggy banks (bearing the name and address of their institutions) to children within their targeted business zones as a reminder to save their pennies. Local political figures hand out reusable carry-bags that people unconsciously walk around town displaying, often unaware that doing so implies an endorsement of the politician. These ideas, as clichéd and low-tech as they are, have been around for more than a half-century and continue to be applied because they still work.

Each is a simple, inexpensive, understated approach to marketing and each provides a physical connection that subconsciously links an insurance agent, bank, or local public figure to the consumer and the community, putting names and logos in plain sight.

The first years of the 21st century were not a great time economically for many of the developed nations of the world. In the United States alone, the world's richest country, unemployment was high, businesses closed, a record number of personal bankruptcies were filed, and uncertainty ruled the financial markets. Yet thousands of new businesses were launched; Internet commerce, still in its infancy, expanded and soared with roller coaster speed; and people continued to make purchase decisions based on a wide range of marketing programs.

As dark as the days were for some, it was a great time for marketers who chose not to give up.

Marketing, once synonymous in the minds of much of the public with selling, has evolved and matured, having a rich history of inventive and successful campaigns, tested and proven techniques and methods. Creativity has never been more welcome, nor has innovation been more embraced and rewarded.

The Power of the New

Being first to reach the market with something new—and a new way to present it—makes reputations and, sometimes, even legends. But seasoned marketers know that many "formula" approaches to marketing a company or organization's objectives should not be discriminated against on the basis of age. They can still be called upon when appropriate to produce predictable, substantive results.

But like any industry, marketing has its risk-takers—the "mavericks" who delight in tweaking traditions and breaking established rules, opting to test concepts that are *new* and *different*—two words marketers like to believe they invented. When the rule-breaking risk-takers succeed, they are rewarded handsomely and are often hailed as industry stars (or flavors-of-the month) or, in the case of an agency, identified for weeks in the trade media as the reigning "hot shop." Looking back, many of the big breakthrough ideas involve slight variations on tested formula ideas.

Marketing is a science that relies on demographic and psychographic studies, considers the uniqueness of various market segments, and employs highly focused methods to appeal to specific lifestyles and different ethnic, religious, socially conscious, and otherwise related groups that are distinguished by factors such as age, income, gender, geographic or regional ties, hopes, dreams, and fears.

In even the most challenging economic times large segments of the public still buy homes, cars, clothes, toys, electronics equipment, sporting goods, food, fragrances, bicycles, and candy bars. They vote, go to movies and concerts, join clubs, and take business trips and vacations. Their choices, whether or not they realize it, are strongly influenced and ultimately determined by carefully conceived and well-crafted marketing programs. This is true of even the most intelligent and educated consumers.

And many times throughout the process, decisions are greatly colored by a consideration that has long enjoyed both high visibility and great power among all levels of consumers, regardless of category: *What's new.*

Indeed, some people, when making purchase decisions, from clothing to shampoo to storm windows or artificial flowers, are *only* concerned with what is the newest or latest version, edition, or alternative to their previous purchases. For more than a half-century, the words *new* and *improved* on packaging reflect not only a marketer's desire to position a subject as fresh—and therefore make it competitive with both other established brands as well as the most recent market challengers—but to offer a response to consumers' real, perceived, or, in many instances, *created* demand.

People who claim to have favorite products and brands insist they are favorites for a variety of good reasons. Yet, the public consistently shows itself to be extremely fickle in this regard, often being drawn to the newest, most lavishly promoted, or most visible alternatives.

Despite a professed appreciation for something of proven worth, it is very often the products with the *newest features*, the candidate with the *new ideas*, the band with the *new sound*, and the drink with an *all-new taste* that challenges the public's loyalty to old favorites, trumping products of known quality, reasonable price, and high satisfaction ratings, all with the simple claim that it's *new*.

Logic and long-standing cultural tradition holds that what is new is good—in many instances, *better* than what it has been created to replace—or there would logically be no justifying its introduction.

Old, on the other hand, is perceived as bad.

Old will die or retire from circulation, thus becoming a less marketable factor when attempting to bring forward and further develop products, brands, causes, issues, or other subjects. As proof of this, note that in most circumstances when the new version of virtually anything is introduced—from peanuts and low-fat chips to pop stars—the previous favorites seem to disappear. They are phased out or relegated to a distant place on the shelf or in the catalog, if not to total obscurity.

There are some exceptions. A number of favorites manage to hold their loyal following through the seasons, through continued effort and huge marketing support. Generally, however, Internet service providers, computer programs in their latest numeral-with-a-decimal-point versions, and the computers themselves, are among the most dramatic mainstream examples of products that are typical of the new marketing mindset. It demands products continually reinvent and reintroduce themselves, basically starting over in their efforts to achieve acceptance again and again.

Some marketers suggest a devious, subliminal factor is involved in the process as well. That is, to infer to the consumer that those who continue to choose their old brands are themselves old and, by implication, worn out, obsolete, or in a rut. In a culture that equates virtually anything new with energy, fashion, vitality, desirability, and added value, someone choosing the older product is announcing that he or she is out of step with what is currently in style and in favor.

Note how rarely people are acknowledged, much less complimented, for wearing clothes or hairstyles that are familiar, even if they are still appropriate and flattering.

New is often regarded as the very reason marketing exists. When the product or service is *not* new, it is the marketer's challenge to keep it appearing so in order to remain competitive.

Businesses need to keep customers coming back, but they also need new customers if they are to survive and grow. While being *new and different* or *new and improved* might maintain the attention of the customer who is having a difficult time accepting the idea of getting by with last year's version of the garden hose retractor with the built-in MP3 player, it is marketing in one or more of its many forms and disciplines that reinforces to the masses the range of values and benefits that might have otherwise gone unnoticed. This provides the reasons for staying with something familiar and satisfying as well as for trying something new.

Marketing is about getting and keeping customers,

members, contributors, and supporters through the most effective means possible. Advertising, public relations, direct mail, direct marketing and/or online messaging—whether it is described as *affinity marketing*, *relationship marketing*, *experiential marketing,* or by a newer term du jour—is no longer a process of simply delivering a sales pitch or a press release. The medium of communication might change, but the process is still *marketing.*

What qualifies as the latest in assorted bells, whistles, shiny buttons, and bows are all nice cosmetic touches for those consumers (and *marketers*) who have the budgets and the desire for such things. At the core, however, must still be a well-grounded idea and a plan.

Clearly in an ever more demanding and competitive environment, reaching and connecting with a target audience requires more than increasing the ad budget (and adding to the ad clutter) or otherwise enriching the cacophony of messages to which the public has already, to a great degree, become immune and indifferent.

In its most contemporary applications, traditional marketing has evolved by necessity to become *the marketing experience.*

Jane Zarem, writing on "Experience Marketing" for Folio, quotes Tim Sanders, of Yahoo! ValueLab. The director of the San Jose, California-based think tank, insists that, " 'Experience' is the basis of a new economy . . . Whether you make a product or sell a service, what you really need to do is stage an experience that's memorable and compelling."[3]

Mr. Sanders offers the example of Forbes.com, the highly successful business publication's online edition, about which he notes, "They leverage what they have, which is their editorial influence, to create live events or to stage interviews online."[4]

Steve Johnson, managing editor of Forbes.com, focuses on providing a compelling customer experience for visitors to the site. He notes, "Live webcasts of the dozen or more events the Forbes conference unit produces each year represent just one example of the 'experiences' Forbes.com stages for its online audience. Typically two- to three-day events, with big-name speakers and the Forbes brothers usually in attendance, each entire conference is available, as it occurs, on the web site at no charge. People can visit and observe all day long. And it's archived, so they can come back and view it later. Using Internet tools, people can even participate in votes."[5]

Becoming Part of the Product's Life

A marketing experience is often confused with merchandising. An imprinted T-shirt or a cap bearing a company logo is brand marketing. It is not an experience. While tied-in brand merchandise is often a *part* of creating a marketing experience, the process is certainly not limited to that. It is also possible to have a marketing experience that does *not* include merchandising and operates on a largely emotional and psychological level.

Most of the several million children who wore Davy Crockett coonskin caps and fantasized about being "the king of the wild frontier" in the 1950s did not realize they were not unique in their imaginings and that they were in fact responding to stimuli in the form of a carefully-devised and brilliantly executed campaign that not-so-subtly created a union of cap and childhood fantasy. The powerful marketing effort mounted by the Walt Disney Company went beyond what had been previously attempted on such a scale. It did not so much reflect the historical frontiersman Crockett as it did the Disney Studios's version as offered in a four-part TV mini-series, a feature-length film, a complete line of western-style children's clothing, phonograph records, storybooks, comic books, coloring books, lunch boxes, pajamas, toys, trading cards, drinking cups, backyard tents, and assorted other line extensions.

Disney's Davy Crockett was more than a film studio property or even a franchise. The marketing campaign was a childhood *experience* for millions of children. There had been Mickey Mouse T-shirts and watches, Roy Rogers lunch boxes, Little Orphan Annie secret decoder rings, and countless other merchandising extensions of popular copyrighted TV, film, and comic book characters, but never had such a varied and sweeping array of items so caught the fancy of marketers and the public alike. It showed what was possible or, perhaps more importantly, that almost nothing was *impossible* when it came to creating opportunities for marketing experiences.

Through the years the Disney organization has been credited with setting the standard for licensing, merchandising, and marketing methods of extending a brand to touch virtually every aspect of a young consumer's life, from toothbrushes to theme park rides, "official authorized" clothing, and more.

Rarely known to miss an opportunity, in 2003 the company reversed its usual course and produced a highly successful movie based on its decades-old theme park ride, "Pirates of the Caribbean." The movie then served as the catalyst to create a full new line of branded merchandise and licenses for hundreds of *Pirates*-related items. Were these extensions of the movie or the amusement park ride? For executives at two separate Disney profit centers, it didn't matter.

Movie tie-ins, as a form of mass merchandising, had become a $15 billion industry in 2003. Examples of what is possible in creating consumer experiences around products and brands are in no way limited to movies, children's merchandise, or even just to the entertainment sector. Any subject—even intellectual property—could be somehow expanded into a mass-market sensory experience.

Years after Davy Crockett taught little boys around the world a few things about fantasies, Hugh M. Hefner's *Playboy* magazine launched an advertising campaign aimed at attracting new subscribers—in this case, *big* boys. The classic ads posed a simple question that positioned the product and reverberated through the American culture. Ad copywriters, like lawyers, know not to ask a question to which they don't already know the answer. This one was, "What sort of man reads *Playboy?*"

A casual glance at the photos told the story. The models in the ads were all handsome, suave, apparently sophisticated, successful men who seemed also to be, perhaps most importantly, very pleased with themselves. Conceptually the technique employed was a basic advertising technique, creating scenes that appeared to embody elements consumers most desire and encouraging them to wonder, "Can I see myself in this picture?"

Since *Playboy* traded on fantasy in such a major way, it was not much of a stretch for men viewing the ads to indeed see themselves in the picture, reading the magazine, using all of the products advertised in the magazine. They were, after all, the accessories of the *Playboy* lifestyle that helped serve as magnets for the most beautiful, desirable women. Today, of course, such a strategy would appear laughably *un*-cool. At the time, however, *Playboy* was not only redefining the category of men's magazines, it was offering Mr. Hefner's personal philosophy for success. It was the offstage authority on coolness dispensing advice on how to succeed. At its peak, the magazine sold more than 4 million copies every month—at a cover price considerably higher than that of its closest competitors.

What the *Playboy* ads offered the male of the species, a richly photographed series of ads for Blackglama Furs offered women—a momentary escape into a fantasy. Some of the most instantly recognizable and glamorous women in the world were featured in elegant ads, under the headline, "What becomes a legend most?"

The ads had virtually no copy, only the headline and photograph of the famous (if not literally *legendary*) woman, and the brand's logo and signature. That was enough. Each pictured woman wrapped elegantly in fur told a richer, more alluring story than any copywriter might have written. A note planted by company press agents in selected media suggested that the famous women were permitted to keep the furs as payment for appearing in the ads.

Few people ever considered that the women were prominent enough that they could well afford to buy the coats. The point was that the furs were so desirable even women who had achieved the status of "legend" would covet them. And the question left for consumers to answer was, "Can you see yourself in this picture?"

Would the woman who was the marketer's target of the ad want to see herself wrapped in fur? Could she see herself in that picture? Could she imagine herself as a "legend" alongside the other glamorous women in the photos?

If the answer to any of these questions was yes, the ads succeeded. The marketer's fantasy—or rather, *objective*—is to create a sensory psychological marketing experience in which the consumer, as part of the targeted market, indulges herself. For a moment she enters the ad, visualizes herself in the elegant fur coat, imagines living the life of a legend, identifying the image with the product, the brand, and herself.

Every woman will obviously not rush out to buy a Blackglama Fur, but every woman is not the target market for the ad. Marketers are betting that a satisfactory number of women *will* plan, save, and have a goal of one day making the fantasy moment real. And at that moment, nothing less than a Blackglama Fur will do.

Would a man allow himself to experience a

moment of fantasy by feeling, thinking, and believing a subscription to *Playboy* magazine would take him a step closer to a new swinging life? Maybe some men will. But the majority of subscribers and potential subscribers understand that "the kind of man who reads *Playboy*" is in fact any man who enjoys the type of photos, articles, interviews, ads, and, yes, even an occasional moment or two of fantasy.

Advertising suggests to the members of its target audience that what might indeed seem to be impossible dreams today are in fact possible. For more than a century marketers have routinely sold fantasies as the first steps in selling products. One veteran marketer describes the process as giving the consumer "permission to believe" that anything is possible, a belief principle that is expressed in various writings and teachings accepted by millions of people around the world—people who do not perceive the process as part of "being marketed to."

Marketers count on people connecting with their messages and deriving or experiencing at least a momentary sense of great interest, fascination, curiosity, excitement, pleasure, or satisfaction.

But like the new car's mileage, the degree to which the consumer will actually sense, feel, relate, or connect such thoughts to the product, brand, or subject of the marketing effort will vary. Pop psychology promises consumers that the more intensely they visualize their desires as reality and the closer they put themselves to what they want, the closer they will be to actually getting and having what they want.

Visualize it. See yourself in the picture. Buy the product. Sign on for the cause. Follow the dream.

Marketers who view their work as serious business, grounded in solid, measurable principles and facts might dismiss such theories, but variations on this formula have been employed over decades on behalf of countless products and brands—from bite-size pieces of candy to trips around the world. Marketers had only to create the *promise* of a particular experience to convince consumers making specific product choices might change their lives, from simple pleasures to greater comfort, relaxation, or self-esteem. Consider some simple advertising phrases:

- *M&Ms melt in your mouth, not in your hand.*
- *Hertz puts you in the driver's seat.*
- *Wonder Bread helps build strong bodies 12 ways.*
- *Fly the friendly skies of United.*
- *Wednesday is Prince Spaghetti day.*
- *Go Greyhound—and leave the driving to us.*

- *UltraBrite gives your mouth sex appeal!*

Each line suggests a mental picture of an "experience" occurring between consumer and product. Again, an ad is not an experience, but the mental exercises the ad can trigger can be very powerful and have, in many instances, as great an impact as the experience itself.

With regard to the *Playboy* magazine and Black-glama Furs advertising campaigns, is it really so easy? Do marketers only need to create great-looking ads with striking visual imagery suggesting that if consumers "visualize being the people in the ads" their lives will be transformed and they will actually become all they want to be? Is that enough to launch, position, and sell simple personal indulgences, such as candy and magazines or big-ticket luxury products?

Well, no . . . but many marketers find it a smart way to start. But in the cases of the two advertisers named, both were conducting marketing efforts that went beyond only advertising. It is easy to slip into the pattern of thinking that advertising, public relations, billboards, and direct mail are marketing. They are not. Separately and together, they are components or parts of the larger marketing effort.

For all the research that suggests the most desirable demographic targets for marketers are bright, sophisticated, well-educated, and aware of the multitude of choices available to them, is reaching the market as simple (or simplistic) as perhaps it was in the days when *Playboy* magazine was a good example of the hottest name in its category—a category that, like *Playboy* itself, has undergone a myriad of changes? Marketers rarely find their greatest successes come simply or easily. The process still involves more than luck and timing and depends heavily on knowledge of markets, their histories, characteristics, and trends.

Good creative work has traditionally been what wins accounts for ad agencies, what distinguishes one agency from another, and what sets products apart in the minds of consumers. But in defining creative parameters, many marketers still often openly disagree about what is real and what appears to be less than real—or even to be smoke and mirrors.

The Public, the Audience, and the Crowd

Creating a marketing experience is about engaging and/or interacting with a targeted group, usually with the objective of selling a product or service or of advancing a message or cause, or of generating interest and support for an issue or subject. Whatever the focus of the effort, it is about persuading, convincing, and winning over people, whether individually, in small groups, large groups, or masses.

But different people respond in different ways to

different types of stimulation or motivation. Some are totally passive and choose to remain observers; others are slow to come on board; still others respond enthusiastically, creating a level of energy that seems to be contagious, perhaps even moving a crowd to frenzy.

But does the same method or process prove effective when used to reach a mass market as it might with a single individual? The first rule is, when talking to one person up close, lower your voice. More seriously, if the message is right and well presented, people pretty much respond the same way in large numbers as in one-on-one conversations. There is, however, a certain dynamic that could be termed crowd psychology or even a mob mentality. That is, in addition to experiencing his or her own reaction to a particular message, a person tends to be sensitive to how other people react to the same message, particularly for affirmation. It is truly easy to become swept up in the excitement of the moment. It is odd to attend a concert in a large hall on an evening when the concert is not well attended. Applause seems scattered, almost self-conscious. Audience members often feel uncomfortable being there. When only a few people laugh in a crowded theater, was it because everyone else failed to get the joke or were those who laughed the odd ones?

An audience attending a live performance might be

strongly engaged on an intellectual or conscious level with the performers, but the traditionally passive role of an audience—to simply sit and watch what's going on isn't considered an *experience*. Though some people would disagree.

- A person watching a movie that strikes a deep personal note might be moved to tears. Despite the barrier of a movie screen and the presence of hundreds of other people, a very personal experience takes place.

- What if a show involved a degree of audience participation—audience members standing, clapping along, singing along, somehow actually participating in the moment, becoming caught up in the energy?

- Or what if the audience is a church congregation, following along with the service, responding and continually interacting with the clergyman, choir director, and other participants—literally becoming an integral part of the church service?

- Or what if a crowd gathers at a political rally and interrupts the speaker with applause or shouts of support or agreement, culminating in a vote? Wouldn't that qualify as an experience? Certainly it would.

But would it be a *marketing* experience? If a primary objective of marketing is to convey a message that will ultimately help sell a product, instill a belief, or win supporters, then the principle is the same as a clown performing magic tricks at a children's party or a department store cooking demonstration where volunteers are brought up from the audience.

Call-in radio shows and music programs that invite and accept phone calls from listeners become *active* experiences for the callers, but remain more *passive* experiences for the larger mass audience.

Some plays, such as the long-running comedy *Tony & Tina's Wedding,* invite members of the audience to act as guests at a wedding. Other shows, such as *Shear Madness,* ask audience members to vote on how the play should end.

Radio dramas, often referred to as "theater of the mind," allowed listeners to visualize the drama playing out, making each audience member's mental picture of the experience clearly distinctive from those of everyone else.

The challenge to marketers is to engage with the public, separately and en masse, realizing that resources must be channeled wisely to reach the broadest possible market, yet knowing that people find different things funny, scary, entertaining, useful, offensive, or boring. To touch people individually at some level while they are part of a crowd, an audience, or the public requires skill and creativity and, as daunting as the task may seem, marketers do it successfully every day.

When Experience Becomes "Experiential" . . . or Not

The term *experiential marketing* has prompted at least some confusion and more than a little disagreement within the marketing community itself. While creating an "experience" for the consumer should be to at least some degree an aim of most marketing programs, does—or *should*—every such experience fall into the category of *experiential marketing*? The answer apparently depends on who one asks.

Dr. Augustine Fou, founder and CEO of the New York-based marketing services, technology, and consulting firm Marketing Science, notes that, "Car ads which show good looking people driving around to pop music depict the experience one can expect to have when driving that car. But consumers seeing the ad on TV do not have that experience themselves; they are merely watching someone else have it on TV . . .

"The impact of such ads on consumers and the likelihood of it motivating a consumer to take some action is low. Victoria's Secret's famous TV ads which feature beautiful models lounging

*around in their lingerie depict the experience
one would have if one wore their lingerie. But
these ads are hardly what we would call 'experiential marketing' since the viewer of the ad is
merely a voyeur who has not experienced the
product themselves."*[6]

Dr. Fou cites several examples of advertising to
which he believes the term *experiential marketing* has
been misapplied, including:

- A "Tide Mountain Fresh" television spot de-
picting images of meadows of flowers and
snow-capped mountains—two scenes rich in
direct sensory appeal that evokes outdoors
experiences.
- AT&T's "reach out and touch someone"
campaign that has emotional pull by alluding
to the warm feeling people experience when
talking to really good friends or people they
love.
- Polo TV commercials showing apparently
wealthy young people on horseback, playing
polo and enjoying themselves at their Hamp-
tons estates, driving expensive cars and
speedboats as inspiring music sets the tempo
of a wonderful life.

- Sprint ads for the company's picture phone in which someone sends an instant picture of a pig drinking cappuccino.
- Other ads for Sam Adams Light beer and Burger King fast food restaurants in which colorful experiences are depicted.

There are of course many good examples of ads that stir strong emotions. The argument appears to be that the *depiction* of an experience—as much as it might evoke an *image* of an experience—is not the same as the experience itself, thus these should not be described as *experiential marketing.* This certainly seems to be a reasonable argument. Otherwise, it follows, people might be content to view or receive postcards of Paris, believing they are as good as visiting the city itself.

What is commonly termed *experiential marketing* in the strictest sense seems well placed in a classroom or academic discussion where grids, schematics, references to Greek mythology and holistic experiences, as well as directional, convergent, divergent, and associative *"THINK"* campaigns and concepts are not only discussed but diagramed. But in the real world, little diagramming takes place. Effective, successful marketing programs that establish a bond or connection with the audience and leave an impression that can be tapped at a later date are the result of well-conceived plans and good creative execution. A big idea, if it happens, is a bonus.

The fact that some marketers have created and presented the examples Dr. Fou referenced, judging them by *their* standards as so effectively *suggestive of experience* as to qualify under the designation of *experiential marketing,* indicates that either the classification is itself confusing or perhaps is simply too narrowly defined by some practitioners' standards. In the grand scheme of world peace—or in this case, trying to create a solid and effective marketing program, generate awareness of a product or subject, and evoke a positive emotional connection to it among consumers—how important is this?

The correct answer is probably, *not very.*

As with so many aspects of marketing, professionals define terms based on their own theories, experiences, perspectives, beliefs, or frames of reference.

An often-repeated story holds that if you give a manager with an MBA a choice between spending a million dollars on advertising or using the same million dollars to study the *feasibility* of advertising, the MBA manager will pick the feasibility study over the ad spending option every time. In the course of learning about marketing, lab time is valuable to learn what works and what's overrated. Once the meter is running, however, and the marketing budget has been tapped, marketers need to devote greater energy to creating effective marketing programs and less time to developing progressively more impressive theories of marketing to debate.

What technically might qualify as *experiential marketing* can be left for the academic community to debate by those who care to debate it, but virtually all marketers must regard the process of actually *creating a marketing experience* as a priority and set about engaging consumers in this way.

Clearly some purists believe the "experience" must be physical and interactive and when that's possible, few would likely oppose the idea. But process terminology notwithstanding, history has shown the marketing experience can also occur on a psychological level, quite effectively tapping into emotional or sensory feelings, nostalgia, personal sentiments, daydreams, fantasies—whatever causes the consumer to identify with the subject of the effort. In the 1990s it was forecast that "virtual" experiences, from conference and trade show participation to international meetings, would replace the "actual" experiences with no loss of a sense of richness to the participants. Companies such as WorldCom promoted the concept and all but began selling tickets.

It didn't happen. Either the concept was ahead of its time or reality was not able to catch up to the vision. Perhaps one day such a futuristic experience will be part of everyday life and business. But if the past hundred years is the basis on which advancement occurs, the "virtual" experiences will be *in addition to*—not instead of—actual experiences. Distance learning, for example, is a concept that is succeeding as an alternative in many cases to on-site classroom participation, but it has not *replaced* classroom learning as the preferred method of educators.

Often what is represented to be an example of the marketing experience is little more than a staged audience-participation event that, while dramatic at the time, does little to create the type of real connection or relationship between the consumer and the product or subject, much less the brand loyalty (and brand equity) that more imaginative, emotion-oriented efforts attempt to induce.

Today's marketing environment operates on many levels, both in practice and in the very physical sense. That is, the consumer, as part of the target market, can be the subject of a variety of marketing methods—and experiences—while:

- In a retail store.
- At a conference, concert, meeting, or other event.
- In an educational environment, such as a school, museum or gallery.
- In transit (in a car, on a bus, plane or train).

- Surfing the Internet.
- At home alone.

Certainly the live, multi-sensory activity that occurs upon entering any of a number of unique, special interest clubs, parks, theaters, businesses, or other locations (such as the Disney stores, American Girl stores, Niketown, IKEA, or even a local Starbucks) produces an experience and physical connection that would be difficult to match with even a great print ad, a dazzling direct mail letter, a CD-ROM, pop-up, or radio's best attempt to create a "theater of the mind."

But there are often instances where a physical connection is simply not realistic and is therefore not an option. People in Kansas, for example, might want to be part of the American Girl "experience" but, at this writing, the company has stores in only Chicago and New York. For the millions of potential customers outside these two metropolitan areas, exploring alternatives for attempting to create a marketing experience seems the only viable option.

Obviously not every person responds to the same marketing messages and marketers must appreciate that one message is not right for every segment of the total market. Market research can provide data as to what works most effectively with different market demographics and segments.

Many marketers have often confused noise with

creativity, as if being loud were the equivalent of being creative or innovative. While some specialty stores aim to provide "the ultimate marketing experience," their methods can sometimes be overwhelming to certain types of consumers. Creating a connection between the product and those who compose its target market does not require a pump-up-the-volume theme park atmosphere.

The *Playboy* and Blackglama advertising campaigns were both very understated, but were also very effective, first in creating a fantasy and a mental picture of what could be; then at prompting the consumer to go on to the next step, promoting a physical image that brought the consumer into the product's space.

As some adherents quite understandably hold that ads alone, regardless of their creativity and popularity, do not constitute an "experience" on the part of consumers, others maintain that's not necessarily the case and advertising is, at the very least, the first step in the experience process.

Again, Marketing Science founder Dr. Augustine Fou contends,

"Experiential Marketing is the difference between telling people about features or benefits within the confines of the thirty-second TV spot and letting them experience it and get their own 'a-ha' event."

It is highly unlikely anyone will buy a fur coat solely from seeing a photograph in a magazine, but the advertising photo puts the image in the consumer's mind. Once it is there, the consumer is encouraged to imagine how the coat will look and feel and move, where it will be worn, how others will likely react. Can such imaginings or visualizations qualify as a marketing experience? Perhaps not in the "experiential" sense, but there are those who would argue that an impression being made strongly enough that a product becomes part of a consumer's consciousness is indeed, *a marketing experience.*

For decades, smart marketers have cultivated the potential richness of the consumer's imagination. Just as for more than a century psychologists have used various forms of suggestion to attempt behavior modification, marketers also continue to experiment. Using print ads, TV spots, billboards, and dramatic presentations they invite consumers to stop, look, imagine, taste, feel, explore, and become part of a satisfying experience that will result in decisions in favor of the marketers' products.

Apart from the actual visit to a store and the dream-inducing ad, certainly a well-constructed direct mail package that begins with the simple words "welcome new member . . . " can affect a genuine transformation. A single person standing in a room is no longer alone, but a "member" and perhaps even a highly coveted one at that.

Such an understated greeting creates a change in status, a feeling of acceptance, a connection to something larger, perhaps something greatly respected or even highly prestigious. It creates subtly through association, *a marketing experience* every bit as real to some consumers as an induction ceremony held in a large, crowded hall.

Similarly, with the simplest application of technology, specifically a person at home alone with a PC or laptop computer, can complete a form, enter a password, and both become and *feel* a part of a previously closed or private "exclusive" group of members, patrons, or guests who might physically be in a particular location, in another town, or on the other side of the world. The payoff could involve interactive communication via chat rooms, virtual or visual tours, or simply access to material otherwise not available to members of the general public.

Marketers will be hard-pressed to convince computer users who accept the premise of "virtual reality" that what they see and do in cyberspace is a lot less than real. To many of them, it is *better* than real and, at the least, exciting.

The *marketing experience* may also involve an "exclusive" opportunity to directly sell products that may or may not be otherwise available, offered at special rates to only special "authorized" buyers or members.

To much of the public, the promise of the Internet was an information superhighway meant to be traveled, a world without borders, streaming video, "instant messaging," the ability to communicate—to see and hear concerts and conferences, events and presentations, fashion shows and film festivals, tours and auctions, in real time.

For marketers, the Internet provides the ability to market on the most grand and massive, yet personal and individual level to anyone anywhere in the world for perhaps a fraction of the cost of maintaining a single showroom in a bricks-and-mortar environment.

The Internet: All for One, But Not for Everyone

As powerful as the Internet is—and its full potential has yet to be realized—it is still not necessarily the first or best choice for every product, service, or issue—or for everyone.

In the late 1990s marketers scrambled to react as virtually all businesses, organizations, and institutions raced to create "an Internet presence." Budgets were cannibalized and funds shifted from proven media to "new media" online.

The problem was that despite great buzz in the

press, where headlines routinely promised "The Future is Here!," the Internet as a medium was still evolving. Reliable data as to who is using it, how they are using it, and whether or not it is, in fact, a viable competitive marketing medium at all is still sketchy.

With the collapse of the market for technology stocks and the bursting of "the Internet bubble" in 2000, Internet marketing efforts—which at the time might have been compared to the careful and predictable course of a bottle rocket—took on a new and distinctly chaotic look. With tens of millions of web sites, hundreds of search engines, and a changing array of ISPs (Internet service providers), the Internet would clearly be a huge factor in providing and furthering information, communication, and education, but *how* it might be used most effectively was still a hotly debated issue. This was especially true among certain demographic segments and if any of those segments happened to be a marketer's main target market group, the vast World Wide Web could be a minefield.

Marketers must always be listening to the voice of the market and be aware of the concerns of the people they want to reach. While *what's new* may be the hot button that gets the attention of consumers in some segments of the market, the priorities of others in the segment may lie elsewhere. Price, quality, and value are the acknowledged, proven determinants for the vast majority of consumers, but how different market segments define those characteristics is relative, begins at different points, and will change according to age, taste, economics, and other considerations.

Beetles, not Beatles

Marketing experiences can be of many kinds, sometimes obvious in their commercialism and sometimes less so. Everyone has probably heard the expression " . . . and they got a million dollars worth of free publicity" applied to individuals, companies, and organizations that become the focus of major media stories and the "placement" seems to occur on an unconscious level.

For years the Beetle was Volkswagen's most popular car—its *signature* model—with much of the public unaware that the company even offered any others. Compact, economical, and appreciated for its functional "ladybug" design, the car became identified as the easy choice of college students and young people on tight budgets. But it was also the preference of socially-conscious people who wanted to make a public statement of their opposition to the much larger "gas-guzzling" cars they regarded as excessive, indulgent, unnecessary, and even offensive from an environmental perspective.

As a class of car, in terms of style, luxury, or dependability, Volkswagen's Beetle was never considered a serious challenger to Cadillac, Lincoln, Mercedes-Benz, or even the Oldsmobile.

The Beetle solidified its association with a younger market by becoming identified with the youth movement and the "flower children"—a growing number of young people advocating a more peaceful world, free of not only war and destruction, but of prejudices and hate, as well as environmental pollutants and consumer excesses.

On college campuses around the world, a popular activity became seeing how many people could be squeezed into a Volkswagen Beetle. The stunt seemed to be performed for fun, but it was also viewed as making a serious case for the small car's roominess and its very functional design—a direct criticism aimed at the people who sought to justify owning much larger vehicles by insisting they were necessary to accommodate families with children.

For some 20 years the owners of Volkswagen Beetles seemed to be telling their fellow motorists and the rest of society where they stood politically on the subjects of consumerism and the environment, even if the car *was* primarily chosen because it was economical.

A web site called *Steamboat Pilot* published a series of human-interest stories, including a report in 1997 that might also have been written two or three decades earlier. Its headline: "Students pile into VW Beetle; set record."

Noting with humor and drama that, "It was a dark and stormy Thursday afternoon," the reporter described a group of middle school kids peering with disbelief through the windows of a Volkswagen Beetle as 34 of their fellow students—layered, packed, and squashed—crammed into a Volkswagen Bug. The paper quoted the students' teacher as saying she thought the "Bug Squash" was a great way for the kids to have a little fun after school.[7]

In 2000, Missy Cummings, professor of engineering fundamentals at Virginia Tech, told a class of incoming freshmen to estimate the maximum number of people that could fit inside a new Volkswagen Beetle. The professor's hope was to spark her students' interest on both an academic and social level. Their responses, complete with formulas and diagrams, ranged from three full-grown people to 112. As the car's advertised capacity was four, how might the matter be resolved?

Professor Cummings offered extra credit if the class could locate a Beetle and test their hypotheses. After cramming and scrunching, one group actually squeezed in 21 people—three fewer than the reported adult world record.[8]

In the 1970s stories such as these were common in newspapers and national magazines as college students across the United States routinely competed for new records (and attention) to see how many people they could fit in a Volkswagen. It was invariably regarded as innocent fun for the students and a great visual story—a photo op—for the media. But for the carmaker, it was a widely publicized, often repeated, and dramatic example of *a marketing experience,* whether the participants squeezing into the car were aware of it or not.

Times Change . . . and Then Sometimes, They Change Back Again

Fads come and go. Public tastes have been known to become more sophisticated and then abruptly shift "back to the basics." As the political and social landscape changed and the flower children eventually went the way of all flowers, the Volkswagen Beetle changed as well. In the United States it took its place in the Peace Museum alongside the anti-war posters and the "protest songs" of socially-conscious folk singers such as Pete Seeger, Joan Baez, and Peter, Paul, and Mary. The car that stood for more than simply transportation disappeared from roadways and the manufacturer discontinued production of the Beetle for the U.S. market in 1979.

Nearly two decades later, as a healthy U.S. economy helped bring about a shift toward greater indulgence and consumption, Americans bought record numbers of "sport utility vehicles (SUVs)." Part truck and part bloated adaptation of the old family station wagon, these larger vehicles signified a general market trend toward bigness. Approximately half of the cars on U.S. roads in the year 2000 were SUVs.

As the strong economy sputtered, however, some consumers looked for alternatives and many of them turned to the past. Some smaller, more economical cars were getting another look. As many people, again on tighter budgets, wished they could go back to simpler times, the Volkswagen Beetle was poised for a comeback.

Marketers understand cycles in fashions. Retro was in. Ads for Alka-Seltzer, Ovaltine, Star-Kist tuna, and other products whose sales had peaked a generation earlier, asked people to "remember how much they loved" these old favorite, once market-leading brands.

Volkswagen introduced a modified, though nearly identical in design, version of the Beetle in the 1990s with great success. The new car cost more, as most products did after nearly 20 years, but it offered added safety and comfort features consumers had now come to expect in their cars. Much of the Beetle's great appeal, however, was in its history and image and of an era now greatly romanticized by a generation.

It brought back a visual representation of a time many older consumers wanted to recapture and a period younger people sought to experience, marked as it was by unforgettable music and energy—an era of excitement and historic change. And the Beetle was presented this time around with the added muscle of a powerful marketing program, more modern packaging, and promotion.

Volkswagen, of course, could no longer position the Beetle as a sort of "little car that could," since the company was now a successful major global manufacturer. But many people in the target market segment viewed the Beetle as both an economy car and a symbol, inviting updated images of "flower power" and of times that were changing . . . and, once again, the people who wanted to could see themselves in that picture. It wasn't a college "happening" in 1970, but it was an emotional connection to a product that was associated with a point in time that for thousands of consumers was still very real.

The old expression, "a picture is worth a thousand words"—and the marketer's adaptation of the phrase, "a word is worth a thousand pictures"—speaks to the marketing experience concept. A photo of a Volkswagen Beetle or a long-haired, bare-chested young person in a headband, or mentioning the words "Woodstock" or "Vietnam" or "Camelot" can inspire images and daydreams of a particular time and place.

An inspiration that makes a person receptive to a sight or sound that results in the purchase of a car, a book of photos, a "treasury of recorded music," or anything that on a subconscious level motivates a change of mood or feeling, is truly or virtually a marketing experience—even if the consumer considers it only a memory.

When a Marketing Experience is NOT a Marketing Experience

Just as there are people who believe that "any publicity is good publicity" (a theory, incidentally, that is totally flawed), some professionals insist that marketers who establish a real-time personal connection with a prospective customer are creating a marketing experience—as if the very act of speaking and listening constitutes a connection. In the simplest sense, that might be true. In reality, it also is not true and two glaring examples emphasize the point: telemarketing and spam.

A marketing experience engages the consumer. *Telemarketing* does that too. It is usually annoying and intrusive.

"Ah yes!" one might shout. "Isn't advertising *always* intrusive? Aren't people now accustomed to seeing and hearing ads that interrupt their routine—breaking into television and radio programs, popping up midway through printed pages, staring down at them on buses and highways, crowding the cable guide and *Sports Illustrated* swimsuit edition in their mailboxes?

Of course. Sometimes ads are even the reason people seek out certain media, such as the Home Shopping Network on cable TV and various fashion publications, especially bridal magazines and books on party planning. But there are certain examples of contacts when the *form* so dramatically overpowers the subject with its deliberate intrusiveness that even some otherwise desirable products and services are hurt rather than allowed to benefit from the process.

A telemarketer places a phone call; the person answers the phone, usually with a pleasant greeting (though certainly that occurs less often since the introduction of "caller ID"); the telemarketer addresses the person by name, with an even friendlier greeting, typically followed by a sincere inquiry about the person's health—as in *"How are you today, Larry?"*

The telemarketer never asks, "Am I interrupting something?" or "Do you have time to talk?" A personal, presumed friendly interaction is taking place, often for up to a half-minute, until Larry growls, "I'm not interested," and hangs up the phone abruptly, leaving the telemarketer in mid-sentence, responding to the person's announced lack of interest by ignoring the comment and continuing to speak.

The controversy surrounding spam—and whether or not it is a legitimate tool for marketers—is even more dramatic, if in a subtle way. An email is also a personal contact and, in many ways, even *more personal* than a telephone call. Unlike phone numbers, email addresses are not listed in a free public directory.

Marketers also understand that people tend to have very personal relationships with their computers—much the same as with their wallets—storing in them confidential information, from unlisted addresses and phone numbers to financial data and assorted material, often considered *so* personal as to be protected by a password never committed to paper. Access to someone's personal computer is about as personal and secure as it gets . . . .

Spam is a personally directed email that became universally despised within days of its creation.

Both telemarketing and spam present themselves as methods of marketing to a targeted public. Telemarketing and spam are classified as direct marketing concepts. Once telemarketing was actually considered a respectable and honest, if somewhat intrusive, way of reaching the public with offers of serious sales opportunities related to real products and services of a kind that people actually want.

That changed.

And when a sales pitch arrives by email,

sandwiched between other email invitations to "see what Luscious Randi looks like with her clothes off!" and "add three more inches now!," it is difficult to take any of the legitimate offers seriously—or to even regard them as legitimate.

Spam is also a major transmitter of computer viruses and is an instrument in the soaring instances of "identity theft"—a 21st century criminal act that relies on thieves having access to personal account numbers and other information.

As a general rule, marketers strive to win friends and influence people, to earn the trust and loyalty of those who compose their market, to build equity and create relationships. Not these guys.

Millions of people have paid millions of dollars to purchase blocking devices that will intercept and pre-empt phone calls and emails from telemarketers and spammers. No other business or industry can claim so much of the public has actually *willingly* paid to keep from being contacted by one of its representatives.

Telemarketers, after years of being the butt of jokes and criticism for calling people at certain times of the day—particularly at dinnertime—when their calls seemed to be most intentionally intrusive, simply ignored the complaints, continued the practice, and appeared even to accelerate it, adding an in-your-face note of persistence.

Spammers send email messages by the millions

each day to a public that has no desire to have its privacy and computer mailboxes violated and have indicated overwhelmingly that it has even less of an interest in the "products" being promoted.

On a typical day virtually anyone with an email address is likely to receive any or all solicitations such as these—*usually several times* in the same day:

- Renters receive invitations to refinance mortgages they don't have and apply for home equity loans on properties they do not own.

- Women of all ages are sent a variety of offers for systems that promise to add inches to their penises.

- Everyone gets invitations to buy Viagra and other products that promise to enhance their sex lives—and at huge discounts.

- Young children, married people, senior citizens, and seemingly everyone else receives information about matchmaking services— including special offers to secure an imported, beautiful young bride who is currently waiting somewhere in a country in Eastern Europe or the Far East.

- Literally millions of people reported receiving unsolicited hard-core pornography via the Internet, usually with a misleading subject title that encourages recipients to open emails that can then be closed only by turning off the computer.

While these are in fact "connections with consumers," they are not "marketing" experiences.

It isn't "marketing" and only serves to contribute to public cynicism and distrust of true marketing programs and professionals. While creating a marketing experience is a desirable goal, clearly all "experiences" are not equal in value or integrity.

The "Bad" Marketing Experiences

Bad news is bad news, however one might try to "spin" the facts. It is not unusual for even well-established and prominent companies, businesses, and professions to experience difficulties at some time or other. Certainly some problem situations seem to "come with the territory" and can be easily resolved, while others can become public relations disasters and result in short-term or long-term image problems and perhaps irreparable damage to an individual or organization's reputation.

There are some professions that start out with a strike or two against them. For example, few people would argue that collection agents, employees of repo companies (people responsible for repossessing automobiles and other merchandise being financed when payments fall far behind), and assorted government bureaucrats, though often performing necessary services, are held in generally low regard by their fellow citizens.

Today doctors, lawyers, corporate executives, members of the clergy, and the military personnel at virtually all levels, have at various times experienced scandals that have damaged the highly-prized images of their respective professions. But in every case, the people in charge recognized the damage done to their reputations and addressed the issue, seeking to change people's opinions of their industries or professions and regain goodwill. Telemarketers and spammers, as noted, sped off in the opposite direction.

Honest people in the direct mail industry care about the work they do and the impressions they leave. They want and need to revisit the people on their lists again and again, to provide products and services of value, raise money for good causes, and generate support for things that matter.

True direct marketers offer incentives to buy, satisfaction guarantees, and represent themselves courteously and ethically to a carefully selected list of qualified prospects. And they rely upon referrals and market research to help qualify their prospects, noting what people like and dislike—including whether or not they appreciate receiving sales calls at dinnertime or unsolicited emails for worthless or inappropriate merchandise or services.

As long as there have been salespeople (or direct mail marketers or advertising people) there has been a certain degree of criticism. No one, however, has found their efforts so intrusive and annoying that members of the public resorted to legal actions on the level of an act of Congress.

Creating a direct marketing experience that insults, offends, or annoys people is not just a bad way to run a business, it diminishes future marketing possibilities for all.

Multi-Level Marketers

Entire books are written on multi-level marketing. It's a complex area that can generate new friends, new contacts, a lot of fun, and has the potential to be financially rewarding. A multi-level marketing business is also an example of creating a marketing experience at a most basic level, creating personal interaction, and establishing ongoing connections. With that noted, the differences in both products and how various companies do business run wide and deep.

To many people multi-level marketing is the very embodiment and definition of the marketing experience. It is a gathering of people examining, sampling, testing, critiquing and buying products, exchanging information, and there is usually cake.

The first hint that a multi-level marketing experience is ahead is when a phone call or a card opens with the words, "You're invited to a Party!" Chances are there won't be any dancing at this party and probably no liquor. There will, however, be cards to fill-out and at some point during the party, guests will be asked for lists of names of friends so that _they_ can be invited to future parties.

Multi-level marketing—also known as Network Marketing, Matrix Marketing, Direct-Sales Marketing, and, to some people, as pyramid schemes and scams. This characterization does not apply to every multi-level marketer. Indeed, some of the best-known and largest organizations in the world run successful businesses this way.

Multi-level marketing is the direct sale of products or services to distributors and sales representatives who are normally classified as independent salespeople, who resell the products or services outside of the traditional retail market. They invite people to their homes—friends and friends of friends—serve something light, and launch into a presentation or demonstration of a product or a line of products. People are invited to buy the products, for which the host receives a sales commission. Then everyone eats cake.

The guests are all invited to host parties of this

type, invite *their* friends, and receive commissions on products sold.

Why then do some states have laws that monitor and limit the activities of multi-level marketers recruiting friends?

The multi-level or network marketing approach is not new and, as a marketing experience, seems as if it should be fun, fairly simple, and potentially rewarding—performing a service by selling good merchandise to friends.

Selling vitamins or cleaning products to friends who visit is not a bad thing, nor is selling or promoting merchandise in a retail store, online, or by mail.

Quality and value should be judged for what they are and a marketing experience should engage a consumer and create a connection because it makes the right points about quality, value, needs, and desires.

Exploring multi-level marketing with a good and reputable organization can be an excellent way to learn about sales, management, and inventory; make new friends; develop and network potential business contacts; and have a good time. Be mindful of the line where business relationships are defined. Sometimes new recruits are asked to invest in a substantial inventory of product, even before it is made clear what the products do, much less how to market them. Support is virtually nonexistent in the form of materials or assistance.

Good companies, in any other category of business, do not open their doors to anyone and everyone, but take the time to carefully recruit and train people, and money begins to change hands when products are sold—not before. Supervision and support is part of the business plan. Simply put, "let the new kid beware." Whether buyer, seller, or the person in between, know the company, its history and reputation over the long haul. If it seems like a good fit, multi-level marketing can be a satisfying way to achieve success as an independent entrepreneur, and each fresh contact is a new marketing experience.

Types and Stereotypes

In simpler times, a product was created and promoted, and advertising told the public what it did and why it was good. It was also priced so people in the product's target market segment could afford to buy it. If the product delivered on its promises, people came back for more and told their friends about it, who told *their* friends about it, and before long the product would be declared a success, having a loyal customer base and equity in its brand name.

Virtually all businesses have had to deal with competition and over time most industries experienced greatly intensified competition, more demanding profit objectives, and an environment cluttered with noisy, confusing messages. In one way or another every product appeared to be number one according to somebody.

But during the same time period, marketers and their advisers have responded to the challenges by developing more mature public relations capabilities and creativity in advertising to produce sophisticated, entertaining messages; generate special effects; and present a variety of sights, sounds, and images that connect consumers to those messages. Companies and organizations, large and small, local or global, whether moving products or acting in the service of a cause, can offer something that embraces the consumer and the marketplace.

After more than a half-century of fine-tuning the concept, the subject of a marketing effort, whether it is a product, service, brand, institution, issue, or individual, must still identify what sets it apart from alternatives or competitors—its *unique selling proposition.*

But during that half-century, the market itself has changed. Shelves are more crowded. Choices are greater. Consumers know more, expect more, demand more, look more closely at what is being put before them, and often challenge even the most established marketers' claims. Most people just believe they've seen and heard the pitch before.

A marketer's message today has to *touch* the audience and, if the audience chooses to do so, it must be able to touch back. Marketers must create a connection and not only make certain the public sees and hears their message, but that they *experience it.*

Summary

- Effective marketing creates a presence, often without consumers even realizing that it's happening. The brand, product, issue, or subject enters consumers' lives and consciousness, to a point where they no longer notice a brand's logo, but know it's there.

- The marketing experience provides a connection, almost subconsciously linking the product, brand, company, person, or issue that is the subject of the effort with the consumer.

- Marketers should understand the uniqueness of various market segments, use demographic and psychographic studies and focused methods to appeal to specific lifestyles, as well as to ethnic, religious, and socially-conscious groups that are further distinguished by factors such as age, income, gender, geographic or regional ties, hopes, and fears.

- Some people believe whatever is new or improved is the lifeblood that drives marketing as marketing drives business. Companies need to keep customers coming back, but need new customers to help them survive and grow.

- Advertising promised the public that fantasy can become reality and dreams can come true. Marketers sell fantasies as the first steps to selling products, a process giving consumers "permission to believe" anything is possible.

- Pop psychology promises consumers that the closer they put themselves to what they want, the closer they will be to getting it. *Visualize it. See yourself in the picture. Buy the product. Join the cause. Follow the dream.*

- The marketing experience is an orchestrated presentation—an event, ad, or acknowledgment—that causes people to relate to the message, connect with its appeal, and experience a sense of excitement, pleasure, or satisfaction.

- Creating an "experience" and a connection with consumers should be the objective of most marketing programs, but all such experiences do not qualify as *experiential marketing*.

- The marketing experience can be psychological, tapping into emotional or sensory feelings, nostalgia, daydreams, and fantasies—whatever causes the consumer to relate to the subject.

Notes

1. The definition of the term marketing is from *Marketing* by Robert D. Hisrich (New York: Barron's, 1990).

2. The American Marketing Association definition of marketing is from the organization's web site, www.marketingpower.com.

3. Quotations attributed to Tim Sanders appeared originally in the Folio online article, "eXPERIENCE MARKETING" by Jane E. Zarem (October 1, 2000).

4. Ibid.

5. Quotations attributed to Steve Johnson of Forbes.com appeared originally in the Folio online article, "eXPERIENCE MARKETING" by Jane E. Zarem (October 1, 2000).

6. Quotations from Dr. Augustine Fou originally appeared online in Vision: An Executive Brief: "Experiential Marketing" on the web site of Marketing Science (March 21, 2003). Additional comments by Dr. Fou were provided to the author in 2004.

7. Quotation from "Students pile into VW Beetle; set record," appeared on the *Steamboat Pilot* web site http://www.steamboatpilot.com (1997).

8. "Putting the Fun Back into Fundamentals" by Dr. Missy Cummings, appeared in PRISM On-line (The American Society for Engineering Education, March 2000).

Defining The Role of Research in the Marketing Experience

A marketing program should not simply be about saying what the *marketer wants* to say, but should create a connection with an audience on the audience's terms. The program should on some level relate to the culture and appeal to the tastes and values of those who compose the target market.

Again, it is helpful when meeting such challenges that everyone is talking about the same thing and not about differing perceptions. A *culture* is made up of customs, institutions, symbols, and achievements of a particular people or group. Customs will vary from one community to another within a city and when the program is global in scope that can be a lot of communities and customs to consider.

Clearly, what is important to a group of people in one community can be unique and very different from what's important to people elsewhere. It cannot be assumed in matters of choices of products, services, or brands that one size fits all. Perhaps one neighborhood (or community or town) is strongly influenced by:

- The presence of a college or university
- A prominent local artists or writers colony
- Seasonal or year-round tourism
- A dominant religion
- A popular local sports team
- A retirement or senior citizens center
- A race track
- A large gay population

- One or more large ethnic groups
- A particular company or industry

Just as Washington, DC, and Hollywood, California, are known as "company towns" because a single industry—the U.S government and the motion picture and related entertainment businesses, respectively—employs so much of the local population and determines the tone, color, and flavor, as well as the economy, of the area. Other cities and communities likely have similar, if not such obvious, driving influences.

If a marketing effort is to succeed—and an effective marketing experience is to be created—its managers and practitioners must take the time to learn about the particular aspects of the culture that might be unique to the area in which they are attempting to do what they do. The way to determine such information is through research.

It is noteworthy, but perhaps not surprising, that many books on marketing today do not even list "research" (or "market research") in their reference or index sections. Then again, if the book is written by a CEO or a certain type of marketing manager, the reasons for this are already known to marketers.

Many (though certainly not all) CEOs, with budgets already stretched and media costs rising, are typically reluctant—even resistant—when it comes to allocating funds for research. Additionally, some marketing managers are uneasy about what the research might reveal as to consumer attitudes and awareness regarding subjects for which they are responsible. To undertake a serious marketing effort and hope to achieve a real connection with the target market, it is essential to *know your market.* Knowing the market, however, does not mean *thinking* that you know the market and making assumptions based on what your gut tells you or, worse, relying on what conclusions came from an afternoon of meditating on the subject. The most important information marketers can have is knowledge of the pulse and temperature of their markets, such as:

- What is the potential size and scope of the total target market?
- Who is the customer or targeted constituent for the marketing message (male, female, or both; child, parent, couple, or family; single person, student, or retiree)?
- What is the target regional or geographic area?
- What is the member of the target market's age or age range?
- What, if any, is the dominant, influential religious or ethnic affiliation of people in the target market?

- What, if anything, is unique about the lifestyle of people in the target market?

- What is the average income of people in the target market?

- Is education, level of sophistication, or technical knowledge relevant?

- Who or what is the competition or alternative to the subject of the marketing effort?

- How is the subject of the marketing campaign (a product, brand, company, industry, association, person, or issue) perceived by members of its target market—alone and relative to competitors or others in the category?

- If the subject of the marketing effort is a product or company, what is its current market share or ranking?

- What is the history, if any, of companies, products, brands, institutions, or individuals who have tried to achieve the marketing goals or status of the current effort?

- What are the current priorities or concerns of members of the target market?

- How do those concerns relate to the company's (or marketer's) mission or objectives?

Three dismissive comments that have been used to build a case *against* commissioning market research and that have been echoed for decades are:

1. Figures don't lie, but liars figure.
2. They can produce research that will tell them anything they want it to.
3. Why should I have to pay to have someone tell me what I already know?

These comments have certainly been validated on a number of occasions and it is true that "liars" can— and have—produced statistical information that supports their cases while ignoring conclusions that do not.

And those people should be ashamed of themselves. The same goes for those who would produce bogus studies and surveys that "prove" they are right when all other evidence indicates the contrary to be true. Some claims purported to be based on research are not as much "fake" as they are exaggerated. For example:

- Can all the companies and products that claim to be number one at something *really* be number one?
- Do nine out of ten dentists *really* agree about

which chewing gum they recommend for
their patients who chew gum?

- Does every politician *really* have polling
  data that overwhelmingly supports his or her
  position?

Don't confuse exaggeration, hype, or an attempt to
put a positive spin on something with actual research.
The same goes for the bogus work pioneered in the
1980s by the so-called "trend shops" that collected
huge fees from many of the top corporations in the
world for providing data that "predicted" such amazing trends as teenagers would like loud music and colorful clothes in the year ahead. Again, that's not
research.

In their book *The Marketing Revolution: A Radical
Manifesto for Dominating the Marketplace,* Kevin J.
Clancy and Robert S. Shulman, then chairman
and president respectively of the highly respected research firm Yankelovich Clancy Shulman, wrote of
"marketing plans based on ignorance compounded by
mythology."

Among the *myths* cited are, "Most marketing research tools in widespread use, including concept testing, product testing, and advertising testing, have
demonstrated reliability and validity" and "Advertising testing, concept testing, package testing, product
testing, and other tools in widespread practice in the

marketing industry have track records of reliability (i.e., if you measure the same thing twice, you'd get the same score) and validity (the tool measures what it's supposed to measure)."[1]

Obviously, for those who oppose either the funding or the reality of market research (or both), these statements provide a reason to smile. The fact that two very accomplished research experts label them "myths" has to make the naysayers add a bit of hand-clapping and a wink to their delight.

But in the words of the stereotyped slackers of Generation X, "So?"

- Market research and testing procedures are not 100 percent correct all the time. Things go wrong. Sometimes errors and pieces of misinformation are of a type that competent, professional researchers are able to recognize and compensate for, sometimes not. No one blanket statement describes every situation.

- People *do* sometimes provide false information to researchers regarding their opinions and tastes.

- Fashions change.

- Alas, unprofessional or incompetent marketers *do* in fact sometimes rig tests to produce desired results—in spite of the fact that such stunts virtually always end disastrously, yielding worthless conclusions, damaging reputations, wasting money, and serving no one's ultimate interests.

Research is a science and, as with other sciences, not every test or experiment is accurate or its results always true or conclusive in the most exacting sense. But consider: An executive announces that he knows something is right because he's been in the business for 40 years and he knows his market—it is his job to sense the mood of the market and he has always been right in the past. His new product is then introduced and it is a failure.

Why?

Had the executive lost his ability to sense the mood of the market after 40 years?

Was he out of touch with the current market climate?

Was the failure a reflection of some outside factor, such as a general economic downturn that soured, if not poisoned, the market for all products?

Certainly some marketers themselves are reluctant to commission research to tell them what their bosses think the marketers are supposed to know already, which is why they were hired to run the marketing program in the first place.

Certainly too, many marketing programs are extremely successful without the benefit of research. Many people also cross streets without looking and do not get injured or killed. The technical term for that is luck and it's a good thing to have, but it is not an especially sound way to manage a marketing program or a business.

Again, from Yankelovich Clancy and Shulman, "America has become a vast databank of customer behavior, and sophisticated methods have been fully developed to extract every nuance of what customers want, will react to, or reject. The art of seat-of-the-pants marketing and the pseudo-science of 'death wish' marketing are about to give way to real marketing intelligence, to marketing as an emerging science."[2]

What "Everybody Knows" Could Be Wrong[3]

An effective marketing effort requires current research information as well as an appreciation of characteristics commonly dismissed as part of "human nature." For example, people tend to make assumptions that they believe are shared by those with whom they have cultural qualities in common. People who think very highly of their own opinions tend to assume that:

1. They are intelligent, so they know what is right—including what is right for everyone else.

2. Because they are right, others should agree with their conclusions and whoever does not is probably not worth worrying about.

Simply put, if the *marketer* thinks it's so, *everyone else* must think it's so. But it's *not* so.

Consider the management approach that urges people to "think outside the box" or the successful campaigns that stress the uniqueness of a particular perspective.

Starting from a position that "everybody knows" or "we can all agree" on virtually *anything*, reflects a lack of clear understanding of a subject or a market, as well as a certain level of arrogance. Knowledge, even knowledge based on hard facts, is often then subject to interpretation. Virtually no single target market is composed of people who are in total agreement about anything. That is why market research is increasingly important and valuable, particularly in a market climate characterized by uncertainty.

Management has to commit to gathering such data in order to make the most informed decisions.

According to Kenneth W. M. Tyson, an Oak Brook, Illinois-based market research specialist, "Continuous monitoring of competitors, customers, suppliers, and other industry forces should be an integral part of the overall strategic management function of companies. Continuous monitoring prevents a company from being surprised. By keeping apprised of industry developments and competitive activities, a company can take appropriate and timely strategic action."[4]

This is only a sampling of the type of information market research can provide. In a competitive environment where creating the marketing experience is even more important an approach to creating business relationships, knowing the attitudes of those who make up the target market, what they want, where they go to look for it, and what special concerns apply, provides a strong argument in support of research.

As streaming video and webcasts become more common in the marketing mix, tracking what consumers want and how best to bond with them can be increasingly complex. An early stage investment in market research can help avoid very expensive marketing missteps in the later stages.

The late 1990s and the early years of the new century brought an era of generationally-focused, demographic, psychographic, ethno-centric, *don't-just-stand-there* marketing programs.

The result of this explosion of communication vehicles is that, at least in theory, people are better informed. For marketers, this is a double-edged sword.

Because the Internet has changed the lives of millions of young people, can marketers assume that if that is the market segment to be targeted, its users have logged on to all the most popular or influential web sites, received emails from assorted special interest groups (and actually read them), and dutifully followed the directives of the various TV channels, programs, catalogs, magalogs, commercials, and packages of every type to "go to our web site for more information"?

Or has the target market, separately or collectively, sat this one out? What is the percentage of a marketer's best prospects that still gets its news from traditional (or "old") media and regards unsolicited email as spam?

For decades intelligent marketers pored over studies and reports that provided indications as to which corner attracted the largest crowd.

Depending on the time of day; part of the world; a person's gender, age, income, ethnicity, political views, health, and social status, the answers ranged from *The Wall Street Journal* and the *Today* show to *Monday Night Football* and Wednesday Night Bingo; from MTV to a book club meeting; church services to the local farmers' market; the mall to the teen center, senior center, or singles bar.

In the digital age, can marketers assume the target

segment they are after has gone digital? Certainly some of them have, but how many?

Research, which has long provided the knowledge that was the power source for so many marketing plans, is even more necessary in the highly segmented and fragmented information age.

The public is as connected to a variety of subjects as it wants to be; it is in more places; interests are more fragmented and specialized. Marketers need to know even more about members of a target market's unique interests, preferences, and concerns before they can allocate their seemingly ever-shrinking budgets.

As the need to create a marketing experience for the consumer grows and the process becomes potentially more costly, the need for information increases and the old objections to commissioning market research become more difficult to justify.

What is the percentage of people that still gather together around the family TV to watch the World Series or the Academy Awards or the Super Bowl game or the Miss America Pageant or the beginning of the New Year in New York's Times Square? How many people still want to watch these events, but view them at the homes of friends, at bars or hotel ballrooms, on Jumbotron screens in gathering places, or on laptop computers? What's the advertising fall-off or the potential for new marketing angles and revenue?

Before a marketing program—much less a marketing *experience*—can be created for consumers, marketers must learn as much as possible about the people who make up their target market segment, their likes, dislikes, interests, concerns, and priorities. Research professionals and firms know how to qualify members of focus groups and participants in surveys, studies, sampling, and testing programs to get the most representative insights from them.

Even when working from a reliable database, a series of qualifying questions typically precedes the interviews or exercises to make certain the information obtained will, as much as possible, reflect a cross-section of people or a narrowly defined group that truly constitutes the market for a particular product, service, brand, company, or subject.

The Research Experience

In some instances research developed to help create the marketing experience can become an experience itself. For example, product sampling, usually positioned as a promotion, is also an opportunity to observe consumer reaction, which, if negative, can lead to changes in the product to enhance both its quality and marketability. If the response is positive, the sampling can be a useful selling point or perhaps the basis of an entire campaign.

In the latter instance, sampling was not only a way of making members of the public aware of the product, but of involving them in an experience with the product and creating a real connection between consumer and product. If recorded for later viewing in marketing meetings, research presentations, or perhaps even for possible use in an ad, the sampling could provide useful information long after the promotional experience ends.

The Pepsi Challenge is arguably the most famous and successful consumer taste test. It pitted Pepsi against rival colas, primarily targeting historic market leader Coca-Cola. Initiated in Dallas, Texas, in 1974, it was useful for the comments it generated as well as serving as an example of a research experience that evolved into a marketing experience.

The long-running "test" became the theme of an extremely successful ad campaign that positioned Pepsi as bold and brash for involving the public in its ads and earned the brand extra points for being confident enough of consumers' reaction to the product to conduct and present the "challenge" on live TV. During the course of the ad campaign's run, some 20 million people in cities throughout the United States took the Pepsi Challenge.

Suffice to say, a lot of testing was also conducted

without TV cameras present in order for Pepsi to become confident enough of the results to not risk public embarrassment or damage to the company or the reputation of the brand.

Further, wherever the Pepsi Challenge was conducted—at shopping malls, outside schools, on beaches, in heavily trafficked business districts—large, bold display kiosks were erected, inviting consumers to *take the Pepsi Challenge!* Wherever these kiosks appeared, consumers lined up in great numbers, some hoping to be on TV, others just wanting a free soft drink, but many more just to enjoy the *experience.* As a promotion it was entertaining and fun, required little from consumers, and involved minimal risk.

Additionally, even if lifetime Coca-Cola drinkers participated in the Pepsi Challenge and chose to stay with their original brand of choice, the likelihood is that they—and the people in their communities and circles of friends—would still remember and share the details of the experience for years to come with the rival Pepsi brand being spoken of favorably.

More than 30 years later, the Pepsi Challenge is still cited for its simplicity and effectiveness and is considered a classic example of a research experience presented as a marketing experience.

Pepsi also had the advantage of having as its advertising agency BBDO, an organization that places a huge emphasis on market research and has historically had one of the most sophisticated internal research departments in the industry. The agency's work on behalf of the soft drink giant produced not only successful ad campaigns, but provided great insight regarding Pepsi's target market.

In one instance, for example, the ad agency developed a Pepsi campaign targeted to 30-year-olds. BBDO conducted a research survey for Pepsi in which cola drinkers were asked their ages. Then they were asked *how old they felt* and *how old they would like to be*. The agency learned that young people tended to want to be a little older and old people wanted to be younger. People who were 23-years-old, however, didn't want to change a thing. A shrewd brand positioning strategy was to "think younger." In subsequent ad campaigns, Pepsi described its product as *the choice of a new generation* and the drink *for those who think young*—sell-points that came from market research and, with good creative execution, provided the basis of two more very successful Pepsi marketing campaigns.

A different kind of "taste test" is routine in the technology industry, but is rarely exploited for marketing purposes. Obviously, testing is critical to new technology products in both hardware and software. After extensive lab testing, the products are routinely put in the hands of favored customers or media people, both of whose opinions and endorsements are sought.

Clearly there is some potential danger in that, if the product is not quite ready for prime time—that is, it fails to deliver all that was promised or expected of it—someone of singular importance to the developer will know about it first. A danger exists in tech testing because marketers are eager to score points and out-shine the competition, so they routinely allow their VIP clients and customers (as well as certain influential members of the trade media) the opportunity to become aware and, hopefully, enthusiastic about the product, occasionally before its time has come.

In many instances it is the VIP who presses for an early look at the new product, promising not to count it against the company if the new product does not deliver to its maximum potential.

But such deals and pledges are not realistic. VIPs who know a lot about the product's potential (and that of its competitors) are likely to have greater expectations than anyone else, be more excited if they get the first look at something that works, and be more disappointed if it doesn't. To promise not to count a product that under-performs as a failure is like trying to un-ring a bell. It's done and is duly noted.

Let the R&D people do what they need to do and avoid subjecting a new product to market tests prematurely. The risks may be too great. An insider's account of a product that didn't work in tests is the story industry people tell over and over again.

Ask the folks at Apple about Newton, the long awaited and much publicized little notebook that, uh, *couldn't*. When the product finally made its debut after numerous postponements, it under-whelmed the market and was an embarrassment to the company for performing below expectations and well below the hype.

Once the lab work is done, additional field research with a list of people regarded as favorable to the company and product will provide valuable feedback, generate good "word-of-mouth" publicity, and produce research information based on experiences that can later be repackaged as case studies for presentation to a larger public.

Stamford, Connecticut-based James R. Gregory, a specialist in corporate and brand advertising, believes research provides the direction or focus necessary "to articulate your corporate mission, to set the right goals, to know the audiences (and) to select the media to best reach your target publics."[5]

There is a strong argument to be made for market research and virtually no really good case against it. The major obstacles to conducting attitude and awareness, customer satisfaction, or competitive analysis surveys are: (1) the inflated ego of the CEO or marketer who already knows all there is to know and doesn't want to risk being proved wrong, and (2) the absolutely reasonable questions, "How are we going to pay for this and can we justify such an effort?"

To the first point, only divine intervention seems like a way out. But to the second, there are answers closer to home:

- As to justifying a research study, review:
  —Sales records
  —Additions and deletions to customer mailing lists
  —Membership growth or declines, noting increases or decreases in walk-in traffic
  —The volume of telephone and Internet inquiries and orders
  —Estimates of numbers of new and repeat customers or participants

  to determine whether or not what the company or organization is doing is working or needs to be changed.

- Trade publications—both in print and online—in virtually every industry and profession regularly update studies, surveys, and reports reflecting the pulse of the market, as well as their own readers' and subscribers' comments as to what they would like to see offered or changed. This information is usually available free from the publishers—or in exchange for sitting through an advertising presentation, which might even be interesting.

- Not free, but not very expensive are the consumer/customer/member/subscriber/citizen hotlines—or designated space on the company or organization's web site—that invite and process comments and complaints, as well as the antiquated, but still reliable "please take a moment" cards in stores and offices and included with regular billings, requesting that people who know or do business with the organization rate the level of satisfaction with its services and share their comments.

Providing direction, setting goals, and making sensible media buys are justification enough for market research. But what is invaluable is learning what the public thinks and how it *feels* about a particular product or subject, if indeed it thinks about the subject at all. Creating a marketing experience places an emphasis on building relationships, but without current market research the process can be by trial and error, a foolish and needlessly expensive way to do business.

Summary

- A marketing program should not simply be about what the *marketer* wants to say, but should reflect the mood and culture of the target market.

- When creating a marketing experience, cultures and customs vary within communities, cities, and certainly internationally.

- Not everyone within a target market segment agrees about virtually any subject. Market research is important, particularly in a market climate characterized by uncertainty.

- Before a marketing program can be created, much less a marketing experience, marketers need to learn all they can about their target segment's likes, dislikes, interests, concerns, and priorities. In the digital age, it still cannot be assumed everyone has "gone digital."

- Research developed to help create the marketing experience can become an experience itself.

- Product sampling is a method of observing consumer reaction with an eye toward making any necessary changes in the product, but the process can also be the basis of a possible selling point or an entire campaign, making consumers aware of the product and involved in an experience that will long be remembered.

- Field research with people regarded as favorable to the company and product can provide valuable feedback, generate good "word-of-mouth" publicity, and produce research based on experiences that can be repackaged as marketing experiences for presentation to the public.

- Market research provides direction, helps in setting goals and making media decisions, and is invaluable in determining what the public thinks and how it *feels* about a product, if indeed it thinks about the product at all.

- Creating a marketing experience places an emphasis on building relationships, but without research the process can be by trial and error, and a very costly way of doing business.

Notes

1. Quotations by Kevin J. Clancy and Robert S. Shulman are from *The Marketing Revolution: A Radical Manifesto for Dominating the Marketplace*: New York: HarperBusiness, 1991).

2. Ibid.

3. Portions of the material in this section appeared in another form by the author in an article, "What Everybody Knows Could Be Wrong," published on the Marconi-on-Marketing web site in 2003.

4. Quotations attributed to Kirk W.M. Tyson appeared in *Business Intelligence* by Kirk W.M. Tyson: Leading Edge Publications,1986).

5. Quotations by James R. Gregory are from *Marketing Corporate Image* by James R. Gregory with Jack G. Wiechmann (Chicago: McGraw-Hill/Contemporary Books,1999).

Crafting the Marketing Experience Plan

A sign that has hung on the walls in corporate sales departments and training rooms for decades reads, "Nothing happens until somebody sells something." It is intended to be a motivator, a mantra, and a fact of life accepted by sales managers for years. It's a good line. But with all due respect to its wise and insightful originator, in marketing—of which sales is a major component—something *unplanned* happening can create a chain of events that are not always in the best interests of the subject, company, or organization at its center—and that includes the sale itself.

What if the size of the sale is beyond the scope of what a manufacturer, supplier, or distributor can fill? What if the sale occurs pre-production, before the product or property is ready or the delivery system is in place? What if the manufacturer does not have sufficient resources to produce the quantity (or quality) of product ordered? These are only a few possibilities in a potentially long list of "what if's." Consider then that before the sale, before the ad, before the press release or an announcement of what is to come, nothing *should* happen until someone makes a *plan.*

Many people through the years have proudly embraced the expression, "I'm a *doer*, not a planner." Such sentiments might be admirable in situations where life-or-death decisions require immediate action, but in business, where so much can be at stake, the phrase can be badly misplaced.

In many organizations management requires an updated marketing plan be submitted with each year's proposed budget. It is reasonable to expect the people in the front office will want to know how the company's money is to be spent.

So each year the ritual begins: the plan is set to paper, circulated, tweaked here and there, is approved by all appropriate parties . . . and dropped into a file drawer, not to be seen again until next year's budget is due. While such a scenario is absurd, it is real life in countless companies. It's not good business and it is certainly not good marketing.

As in many other professions, marketers typically consider themselves to be creative people, inclined to follow their creative instincts. This approach is fine for the creative aspect of the program, but it can be disastrous in the absence of an overall plan to guide the process and bring the creative and operational elements together in a timely, cost-effective, business-like way.

Marketing plans can be as wildly different as the people who write them. Some managers confuse marketing plans with business plans and the result is a very detailed document, rich in footnotes and endnotes, often presented in a clip-binder with tabbed sections, looking as if it could have been written for decision-makers in the investment banking department. Few people could ever swear to have read the entire document from start to finish (including the endnotes), but what's important is that they can remind each other it exists.

Other marketing plans look as if their first draft was drawn on a cocktail napkin.

It is tempting to say the best plan is the one that's most successful, but that's not fair. Like great film directors whose styles range from micro-managing the smallest details of a production to those who step back and let their actors interpret the script in their own ways, there is no one way that is *the* way. The plan must be developed not to please its writers or their supervisors, but to advance the marketing effort and support the goals of the company or organization and everyone involved with it, both inside and outside.

In real life, at many companies large and small, a marketing program is essentially created almost spontaneously. That is, the agenda is created at the start of each day and that agenda—often little more than a "things-to-do-today" list—is what passes for a plan.

Press releases are sent out when there is something to announce; ads are placed for no better reason than to be "out there" with something, visible in the marketplace—to get the organization's name in front of its public; trade show attendance and media relations efforts are hit-and-miss propositions.

In marketing circles, taking a cue from battlefield surgeons, this is known among the seasoned professionals as "meatball marketing."

A marketing plan provides direction and serves an extremely important function, particularly if people read it and use it. A question that hangs over marketers' heads in virtually every company and organization in every industry is whether or not the marketer is attempting to *respond to a need* or is *creating a need* for the product or service he or she brings to market. Such questions have a significant impact on how a plan is developed.

For companies and organizations that recognize its value and take the process of communicating with their constituents seriously, a thoughtfully constructed plan *should be* developed. While it might seem absurd to think any organization would *not* take communicating with constituents seriously, it happens often. Management, hoping to keep second-guessing of its objectives to a minimum, keeps information to a minimum. Employees, investors, and the public learn very much after-the-fact that programs have been set in motion that may have a great impact on them, but their concerns were not solicited or considered. What some prefer to think is exercising decisive leadership, others call corporate arrogance.

Very often, members of management's own team are not consulted until it is too late or expensive to change anything. Engaging the public and winning favor in the marketplace begins with the best and the brightest people with an interest in the subject having an opportunity to contribute their energy and ideas.

Marketing Plan Basics

The six essential elements of a marketing plan are the:

1. Situation analysis
2. Objectives
3. Strategy
4. Tactics
5. Time line
6. Budget

A word that does not appear in the plan but must imbue each section is *flexibility.* Conditions can change rapidly both internally and externally, dramatically altering the climate in which the plan will be executed. A plan that is so tightly constructed that it cannot accommodate changes in the business landscape does not reflect a realistic sense of the marketing environment. Without such a realistic sense, the plan itself becomes severely flawed.

Using this format, the plan's writers and creators can outline the direction and scope of the effort using as little as a few sentences under several bullet points or they can expound at length, providing as much detail and justification as management demands and team members need.

To go beyond a formula marketing program to one that focuses on creating a marketing experience, the plan requires something more. That something is an explanation of how the experience will work, what it will accomplish, how long it will take, and what it will cost. This becomes a key component of the basic plan, not a buzzword-heavy presumed reinvention of the concept of marketing.

A *situation analysis* requires a justification for writing the plan in the first place. What's going on?

- Is the company losing market share?
- Is the brand perceived as tired?
- Are new competitors gaining ground by looking fresh and innovative to the core market?
- Does the product seem to be out of fashion in the current economy (perhaps too pricey or so *in*expensive as to be perceived as cheap or of low quality)?
- Was the celebrity spokesperson for the brand just indicted by a grand jury or involved in some other incident that casts a dark shadow on the organization?
- Perhaps the company and brand are okay, but most of the industry is in trouble and the media are not distinguishing the healthy players from the sick ones.
- Is there a fear or concern that companies

based overseas could hijack the market with lower cost labor and materials?

Any one or more of the foregoing might succinctly describe a situation that justifies calling the troops together, buying them weapons, and turning them loose on the market with a charge to be home by Christmas.

For people who like charts, this is a good place to slip one in, detailing losses or lack of significant growth in market share, revenue, new accounts, etc.

Establishing *objectives* is an essential element of creating a plan. It forces management to be specific in identifying the goal or goals of the marketing effort. Perhaps the goal is to reverse negative or erroneous perceptions of the brand or organization that are thought to be holding it back. Be clear about what is to be accomplished. If the goal is to increase market share, it is important to be as focused as possible, such as aiming to "increase sales by 40 percent over a three-year period," rather than accepting just any increase at all. Vague or general benchmarks make evaluating a program's success (or lack of success) similarly difficult.

Objectives should be realistic and achievable. Aiming to be number one in the industry (or in a specific market), for example, could seem to be achievable, but might be an ill-chosen goal if a competitor runs ads showing that it is number one in some specific single category it declares to be significant. Even your true and valid qualifications will mean little if the public believes that to be considered the best in a class is just a matter of interpretation—or, worse, that the claim is just an exaggeration.

The *strategy* describes outlining the approach that will be used to achieve the plan's objectives. Will market share be increased by acquiring other companies, opening up new markets, launching several brand extensions, or pursuing a merger or a joint venture with a competitor?

Listing the plan's *tactics* provides details on how the strategy will be implemented and this is an area where marketing can show its muscle. Will the strategy to achieve the objectives involve:

- Advertising
- Public relations
- Direct mail
- Event sponsorship
- Creating and conferring a grant or an award
- Adding high-profile respected people to the board of directors
- Developing a magalog (a combination magazine and catalog)
- Launching a special-interest web site

- Targeting specific sectors through new, expanded, or more aggressive trade show participation
- Creating, pitching, and merchandising a series of op-ed pieces or advertorials
- Producing special-interest newsletters
- Organizing a campaign of letters to the editor
- Developing an ambitious new branded publication, a cable TV program, or CD-ROM

The objective tells *what* will be done (such as increase visibility in the target market by 50 percent); the strategy identifies *how* it will be done (advertising in major general interest media), and the tactics spell out the *when* and *where* (full-page newspaper ads on Thursday, Friday, and Sunday for three weeks, coinciding with 30-second TV spots on the same days for the same period of time just prior to the sports report on the highest-rated local news program, and sponsorship of an event that involves a local sports team helping to raise funds for a good local cause). Any such variations using media, events, or programs can be mixed to create the most effective strategy/tactics combination.

The ***time line*** is a sometimes overlooked and omitted part of the plan. In many respects it is a reality check. Is it possible to accomplish what the plan calls for, at the approved budget, with existing personnel, in the allotted amount of time? If not, should the plan be scaled back or perhaps implemented in two, three, or four stages over a specific period of time? Must supplemental funding be arranged? Have benchmarks been included to show how the plan is succeeding (or not succeeding) at specific points on the time line?

Obviously it is necessary to develop a **budget**, which addresses the first question management asks and which almost invariably creates shortness of breath in the executive suite. Most people who do not work in media have no idea what media costs, how it is purchased, and if its value can be measured accurately; under what conditions media rates can be negotiated; and what buying options exist within specific budget ranges.

- What about that trade show item? If the company will be expanding its participation, will it need more than one booth exhibit? More than two? How often do these things need to be replaced after being set up, broken down, packed, and shipped around the country? How many trained people will be required to staff the booth or exhibit (or exhibits)?

- A new publication can provide a versatile platform. What will *that* cost? Can it be on the web site to avoid printing expenses and the soaring cost of mailing?

- Is the final list of tactics going to be implemented using existing staff and, if so, who is going to be covering any other duties or responsibilities those staff members may have?
- Will any of this involve consultants, a PR agency, event planner, additional writers or technical staff, training personnel? If so, are the outside resource organizations' fees for services competitive?
- Can any of this be accomplished in stages, using existing materials, in-house staff, or people borrowed from other departments?
- Can costs be amortized?
- Is the web site expected to be permanent or just for the duration of this program?

Historically, management has shown a healthy respect for marketing and fallen woefully short in funding marketing programs. Notice when revenue drops, the market declines, or the front office embarks on an austerity program, which department takes the first hit.

The lack of understanding of the scope, value, and costs of marketing prompts management to unselfconsciously drop comments such as "canceling two ads in *Forbes* won't matter and—look!—we just saved

$90,000!" or asking if the company really needs a public relations firm or can't one of the secretaries prepare and send out the press releases?

When budgets are tight and getting every dollar is a struggle—which is the reality of most companies and organizations most of the time—it is helpful to review the plan with an eye toward how various activities listed in the plan will benefit specific departments or divisions (other than just the marketing department) and attempt to have those departments become involved in the program and contribute a portion of the funding.

A thoughtful marketing plan that lists what is to be done, when, why, and at what cost is a reflection of efficiency and professionalism. Having to budget the plan realistically, justifying every dollar, and fighting to keep it during a year of roller coaster stock market activity is both challenging and predictable.

Where's the Research?

In the previous chapter the importance of timely research was emphasized. Where then does research fit into the marketing plan? The answer is in any or all of the six basic elements.

- Has research validated the situation analysis or, as written, is it simply what the CEO thinks or fears, based on comments from a dinner companion or in-law? Is it what an unsubstantiated account in a trade magazine said the situation is now or will likely become?

- Does competent research support that the objective is achievable in the allotted time at the stated budget?

- Did research indicate that the proposed strategy and tactics were tried by a competitor in a certain market or by someone in another industry but the comparisons can be justified?

- Does the research provide analysis regarding whether or not the plan addresses the specific interests or concerns of the company or organization's constituent groups or how those groups are likely to respond to the effort?

Planning for the Marketing Experience

In discussing the *strategy* section of the plan several possibilities were offered as to which of the available marketing tools and disciplines might be used to their best advantage in achieving the objectives:

- Advertising
- Public relations

- Direct mail
- Event sponsorship
- Conferring a grant
- Creating an award
- Adding high-profile respected people to the board of directors
- Creating a magalog
- Launching a web site
- Increasing the company's presence at trade shows
- Writing newspaper op-ed pieces
- Generating "advertorials" (a combination advertisements and editorials)
- Creating newsletters
- Writing letters to the editors of key papers and magazines
- Developing an ambitious new branded publication
- Launching a cable TV program
- Producing a CD-ROM

Scanning the list, consider which approach lends itself well (or best) to not just a straightforward, one-way presentation of the marketer's message, no matter how creative its execution might be, but to a *marketing experience*—to some type of activity that would in-volve members of the targeted market segment in ways other than as observers.

If no big idea emerges, please note there are rea-sons why radio stations give someone who is the 15th caller a chance to win prizes by answering a question or why companies run sweepstakes. Formula ideas will not win marketers points for creativity, but pro-fessionals know that many proven techniques can usu-ally be repackaged with a new, or slightly different, twist until the next big breakthrough idea emerges.

The experience should include some reason for the consumer or constituent to want to respond, partici-pate, and be a part of the process.

Typically such experiences include a prize, gift, free sample, or other promotional incentive. Often, the reward is the personal recognition or gratification the participant receives, such as the promotion that speci-fies, *"Everyone who enters will receive . . ."*

People often write letters to the editor or op-ed pieces in newspapers or contribute to telethons and fundraising events as much to see their names in print or hear themselves mentioned on TV or radio as to ex-press their opinions or support. People need, crave, and love some type of recognition in most instances.

The most successful (and profitable) television for-mat formula for more than a half-century is audience participation—a game show, talk show, or "reality" program where the person who is neither a performer nor an expert gets a chance to be seen, heard, acknowledged, or recognized, if only for a brief moment.

- Food companies invite members of the public to submit recipes for posting on the company's web site or for publication in a cookbook or for use in a TV program or ad. Any reward, prize, or payment beyond public recognition can be modest.

- Brokerage firms ask members of the public to manage a "virtual" stock portfolio and the person (or 10 people or 100 people) who outperform the market receive a trip or a T-shirt or their photograph in an ad.

- Automobile companies, dealers, aftermarket firms, or publishers invite people to call their "hotlines" and record stories from the road, promising some will be used in publications or future ads.

- Health clubs, weight loss centers, and fashion salons offer free workouts or trial programs promising personal training or consultation and an acknowledgment or recognition ceremony involving people who reach specific levels of achievement using their products or programs.

- "A Taste of Chicago" brought together a number of the city's restaurants, which offered "sampler" plates or full meals at special prices to thousands of people who gathered together in a festival-like atmosphere. Participating restaurants and visitors were shown both close-up and from afar as all local and some national media covered the event. The technique has been modified, rewrapped, and used successfully in thousands of cities, communities, and social centers.

- Theaters present a daytime "sing-along" presentation of *The Wizard of Oz,* a midnight showing of *The Rocky Horror Picture Show*, or another popular themed or period movie where audience members are invited to wear costumes in keeping with the film's story and, on cue, actually respond to dialogue or sing along.

- "Conventions" of Star Trek fans invite people to come together to share their favorite moments from the TV programs and films, meet people who share their interests, and purchase an endless array of clothes, books, videos, CD-ROMs, games, toys, posters, souvenirs, and other related items (some licensed and "official" and some merely "in-spired by" the subject).

- The taste test; "bake-off"; family night bowl-ing; kids-eat-free; "cook-your-own-steak"; "open microphone" night at the comedy club; strolling musicians taking requests and waiters serenading customers at their tables; employees in costume or "in-character" in-volving and entertaining customers in the exposition and demonstration of products; businesses or malls that bring in clowns, ma-gicians, characters, or celebrity impersonators to interact with visitors, entertain, and pose for photos . . .

New or old, updated or repackaged, the list of possi-bilities is limited only by imagination and, of course, by budgets. A public relations professional or firm, an ad agency, or a clever in-house marketing manager should easily be able to devise several creative execu-tion possibilities.

Options such as an awards program; event or con-ference; a cable TV presentation; trade show exhibit; or almost any type of publishing venture or event that mobilizes people from bloggers (individuals who maintain their own "web logs" or personal web sites) to bicyclists, can be an experience that allows the consumer to become an insider and take a personal role in what the company or organization offers.

Challenges such as this are the reason people choose marketing as a career, to devise a creative approach to bringing a product or an idea to the public and inviting that public to become actively involved. Outside consultants can be helpful if their credentials are in order. This is, after all, a business with careers and investments to be considered.

Working out the timing, the budget, and the mechanics of presenting and promoting what the strategy and tactics produce is an exercise that demands organization and creativity that should go beyond the marketing manager coming up with an idea, a date, a place, and a check requisition. Call upon the best resources and talent available within budget.

Creating a plan for a marketing experience is very much a participatory undertaking that could include sales and marketing professionals, as well as technical, research, legal, and other representatives who need to be involved and/or who can contribute something to the effort. Management should appreciate the team-building aspect of such participation as well as the fact that professionals are being challenged creatively and given an opportunity to develop a stronger personal identification and connection to the company or organization.

When such programs succeed they can be career-making events. The prospects can be intimidating to some people and appear totally unrealistic to others with a serious business perspective. Think of "numbers crunchers."

But consider that the most successful business ventures in recent times in virtually every category, from technology to food services to the performing arts, began with a dream or an idea that involved others to a degree that the enthusiasm and appreciation for the subject generated excitement and momentum. After the idea comes the plan.

Summary

- A marketing plan provides direction and serves an extremely important function, but only if people read it and use it.

- The essential elements of the marketing plan are the situation analysis, objectives, strategy, tactics, time line, and budget.

- As budgets of most organizations are typically strained, review the plan with an eye toward which items will benefit various departments or divisions other than marketing, and attempt to have those departments both become involved and contribute the plan's funding.

- The marketing experience should provide a reason for the public to want to respond, participate, and be a part of the process, such as an offer of a prize, gift, sample, or other incentive, especially the reward of personal recognition.

- Even the most gifted marketers can't know everything about everything. A public relations professional or firm, an ad agency, or a clever in-house marketing manager should be able to develop a list of creative execution possibilities, but outside experts should be brought in to consult if that's what is required.

- Creating a plan for a marketing experience is a major undertaking that should include sales and marketing professionals, as well as technical, research, legal, and others who can contribute something to the effort.

Developing an Ongoing Marketing Experience

Life and Times in Marketing

The people or groups a marketer wants to reach are not so much "moving" targets as they are parts of an environment and atmosphere that appears to be ever changing. If a marketing effort does not deliver the desired results, regardless of its size or scope, the company, client, or organization, its agency—or the entity brought in to *replace* its agency—will typically move quickly to try something else. The era of letting a product or brand develop and build over time is history. The business and social climate and economic realities demand virtually instant success or a policy that demands cut-your-losses and move on.

If the effort *succeeds*, however, the climate is not much better. Marketers' attention shifts immediately to planning what will follow the successful campaign.

It's been noted that some marketing professionals grimace at the use of such terms as experiential marketing, dismissing them as trendy buzzwords and resisting urgings to consider them seriously. Yet the actual practice of creating a *marketing experience* to help build a relationship between the consumer and the subject, is accepted and regarded as an often pivotal aspect of the marketing plan and, as such, is taken *very* seriously.

But what constitutes a pleasurable experience or even simply a *good* experience is not only in the eye of the beholder, but can be subject to environmental shifts and other influences.

Most marketing professionals respect the ability to generate attention and interest in the seemingly ever expanding and expensive production and media marketplace, and consider such talent to be part art and part science. To draw in a segment of the public, creating a physical and emotional connection to a subject through innovative, unique, or exclusive concepts was once the province of creative directors. Now it is everyone's job.

People of certain demographic groups, such as the moderately affluent consumers in the 18 to 34 age bracket that is considered by marketers to be the most highly-prized target segment, are thought by current standards to be generally smarter, usually somewhat more aware or sophisticated, perhaps more skeptical of many often overused advertising techniques and claims, and frequently willing to pay more for products and services they perceive to be of greater value or status. This same group, however, is also inclined to ignore that which lacks "sizzle."

The wide range of media, event, and presentation options available in most categories has made the challenge of connecting with a target market both easier and more difficult. Marketers must be more imaginative, more creative and at times perhaps even more *outrageous* in many businesses once regarded as extremely straight-laced or conservative.

- A financial services company offers a promotion that includes trips to Las Vegas or to an island getaway where it might be presumed seminars on budgeting or replacement cost accounting are not among the scheduled required activities.

• An airline made news in 2003 by designating some of its flights "all-nude excursions"— certainly a dramatic departure from options offered less than a decade earlier when common profanity was censored from in-flight movies.

While not all—or even *most*—marketers go to such extreme lengths, these examples illustrate changing mores and public attitudes that can make what had been regarded as a very good idea seem suddenly out of step with the times. The climate created by highly unusual or well-publicized radical approaches to creating awareness and attracting business can encourage some marketers to "take chances," "push the envelope," or try "cutting edge" schemes that can be explained with any number of clichés. They are often less about marketing than about offering an increasingly jaded public something more than familiar or shopworn (thus less effective) sales pitches.

"The Big Idea" that ignites a marketing campaign and allows it to break out from the clutter and distinguish itself from competitors and other marketers' messages, becomes identified with whatever elements make the program unusual or distinctive, particularly for the fact that it *resonates* with the public.

But a marketing program can be months (or more) in the planning and have a large piece of the budget riding on it. There is little time to savor work well done. A follow-up effort or campaign must succeed on its own and must also expect to be compared to every other successful effort the market has had to consider. The struggle reflects the downside of success. The marketer must ask new questions to determine if the new effort is ready to go public:

- Can the marketer follow the hit campaign with a newer idea— something even bigger, better, and more likely to be successful?

- Does the distinctive campaign or message put the product, brand, or organization "in a box" where all subsequent efforts will be measured against the effectiveness of the first success?

- Shall the marketer regard the Big Idea as the product, brand, or organization's "signature" campaign, believing it to be so closely identified with the subject to make staying with it mandatory until the message begins to look tired, creates diminishing returns, and begins to bore people?

These "what are we going to do for an encore?" questions are the curse of creative people in a culture and a society that liberally bestows awards, then requires its smartest, most artistic, and innovative practitioners to try to top themselves again and again.

Creating a marketing experience that resonates with a target market cannot be a hit-and-run matter. Despite the best attempts at generating brand loyalty, much of the public continues to demonstrate that its attention—and its loyalty—require something be not just good, but also *fresh* and *sustaining*.

Before and After the Big Idea: The Marketing Experience

Some marketers appreciate the value derived from creating a connection with the consumer, but accept that in the absence of a Big Idea—or *before* the Big Idea is discovered and implemented, or *after* the Big Idea has rocked the industry and the marketplace with its breakthrough success, when *another* idea is needed—the solution to the problem might be as close as the building next door or the product on the shelf.

Ideally, the Big Idea will have a respectable and profitable lifespan and not be just an event or happening that dominates public consciousness and soon becomes yesterday's news. Certainly some products, companies, or organizations have ridden the wave of such an event for a good long time. The "Pepsi Challenge" might well be the standard among long-running consumer participatory marketing experiences as it was a promotional event, a research study, *and* a successful marketing experience all under a single theme. It continued even as the company continued to introduce and complete numerous other promotions, campaigns, and events.

The message is that the possibilities are wide open. It is not an unbreakable rule to have one campaign continue as another is tested or rolled out, either broadly or in selected markets. The rule that says a message should be cohesive and the public should not be challenged or confused by competing campaigns is not without some elasticity if the idea has value.

So which will it be?

- A single marketing experience event?
- The campaign that includes some type of interactive subject-to-consumer marketing experience?
- An ongoing program, day after day, year after year, that creates and sustains loyalty and builds equity while keeping the public and the subject product, company, organization, or issue together?

The correct answer is that it doesn't have to be a choice of one or another.

Just as there are small companies and large companies; lawyers and street musicians; tech companies and financial service organizations; home-based private businesses and multi-national, diversified corporations; it should not be expected that one type of marketing experience would be right or appropriate for every subject. One entity might successfully employ several different types of marketing experiences in a short time, while another may find something that works for them and continue doing it unchanged indefinitely.

Five Simple Rules for Getting Started

Include these among the most important rules to guide a marketing program:

1. Devise a plan that reaches the target market on an emotional, psychological, or sensory level *and* make certain to include a "value statement" in the marketing message. If the emotional or sensory approach falls short (as some people resist approaches that ask them to respond immediately or participate on virtually any level), the practical side of

the message—the value statement—should carry the day.

2. Do something. Too many companies, organizations, and people—especially in the high technology cyberworld—believe that "being there" is enough. Do not wait for the public to find your message on its own or come looking for what you have to say, especially while being inundated by unsolicited information that might be too much to process under the best of circumstances. Even search engines offer interested persons up to hundreds of thousands of alternative responses to most requests for assistance. Marketing has a range of weapons in its arsenal that, any one individually or in combinations, can generate awareness, visibility, knowledge, support, or appreciation. Use them.

3. When given the option of presenting a message that informs or a message that *informs and engages,* go with the latter. Telling the story is good; knowing the listener can hear and respond is better.

4. When given the option of creating a marketing experience or of creating an ongoing marketing experience, again, the second

choice is the better of the two. It is the difference between a consumer coming in once to try a product or service and the consumer coming back again and again. It is the difference between wearing something people notice and appreciate once and wearing something people notice and appreciate many times. It is like getting one paycheck versus a regular income—paychecks in the same amount every week or month.

5. Without making the process complicated, involve participants on as many levels as possible. There are reasons airlines offer first-class seating and coach seating. Everyone can't afford—*nor necessarily wants*—the same level of status or luxury. Performers don't all win starring roles, but find satisfying or rewarding experiences in being supporting players, cast members, behind the scenes participants, and extras. Being exclusionary can work against a marketer at different times. It is not unusual for someone entering at one level to move up to another if he or she has a good opinion of the subject and its management.

Market for Now

"Change" is a strong word in marketing as it is often both the signal and the justification for the introduction of new ideas and campaigns. Another word that makes marketers virtually swoon is "timeless." Think of words or phrases used most effectively that carry the power to persuade . . . or to close the sale:

- Diamonds are *forever.*
- *Long-lasting freshness.*
- Beauty that is *timeless.*

Love is *timeless, ageless, undying.* Research would likely give these words and phrases pretty high marks when it comes to listing benefits and advantages. But what if the target market is teenage boys or a personality type that eschews sentimentality and makes decisions based on hard facts and numbers? Timeless is probably not a word that sells.

In fact, the most successful marketing programs typically reflect "the *now*"—the current mood and flavor of the times, even when a campaign employs elements of nostalgia or has a retro theme. From package designs and pricing of products and services to the means by which the message reaches the public and the very phrasing of the message itself, a marketing program must reflect a perspective or sensibility that appears to be appropriate to the present moment and can be easily understood if it is to resonate with the public.

While market research is a key component of most programs, there are times when surveys or studies seem *less necessary* in order to gauge the pulse of the market. The sound of the market is sometimes quite obvious to those who choose to hear it.

Putting a Finger to the Wind and Listening to the Market

Social scientists examine cultures from many perspectives, often segmenting periods named for defining moments, events, dominant attitudes or moods—such as *Prohibition, the Roaring Twenties, the Great Depression, the Jazz Age, the War Years, the New Deal, Camelot, Watergate, Woodstock, the Women's Movement, the Summer of Love, Yuppies, the Information Age . . .*

Since the 1960s, marketing has played a major role in both reflecting and influencing attitudes and trends, often blurring the lines between culture and commerce. Art imitates life, life imitates art, and there is usually a logo, a book, CD, DVD, a ceremony or event, a clothing line, web site, and at least one "recognized expert" to explain it all.

In the early years of the 21st century, a question

(borrowed from the controversial, sometimes notorious, cultural icon Martha Stewart) addressed the growing polarization of various groups and lifestyles, and the commercialization of institutions: *Is that a good thing or a bad thing?* The debate is far from over.

Political correctness, for example, goes in and out of favor. Heightened sensitivity frequently becomes the rule in the workplace, the media, and most definitely in programs devised and developed by marketers (or it should). Concern over not offending any institution or group is constantly evaluated in light of both current public sentiments and changing times.

In the United States, immediately following the historic September 11 terrorist attacks in 2001, at least two major motion pictures scheduled for release had their premiere dates postponed indefinitely. The films' subjects or pivotal scenes included incidents involving terrorism. Just as the start of the U.S. involvement in World War II caused the country—if not the world— to shift gears and reconsider its priorities and values, September 11 stopped the clock for many businesses and organizations in America and around the world.

The day had barely begun when school teachers stopped teaching, businesses sent employees home, meetings were cancelled, airports closed, stage performances and sports events were scrubbed, and all eyes turned to 24-hour television news coverage. The world's richest nation was waiting for news of . . . something. The public hoped for a sign indicating it was okay to begin moving again and, if so, in which direction and how fast. Projects, events, plans, schedules, and budgets were all put "on hold" while they were analyzed, scrutinized, and reconsidered.

In the hours, days, weeks, and months that followed, individuals and businesses made tentative moves to regain their normal levels of activities. People closed ranks, reached out to one another, and asked each other what they could do to help. Most people appeared to be both more guarded and more approachable at the same time.

A few years later, much looked the same on the surface—planes flew, comedians told jokes zinging celebrities and corporations, major designers unveiled new fashion collections, still more flavors of Coca-Cola made their way to store shelves—but the undercurrent of life and commerce conveyed a sharp feeling that everything was somehow different. People looked at the skies, not actually knowing what they were looking for, but knowing that in a second life could change again.

So what does a terrorist attack have to do with marketing? While the example may seem a bit extreme, a terrorist attack, a hurricane, a national period of mourning, or a corporate scandal are only a few unexpected developments that can put a marketing plan, a budget, or an entire organization in freefall.

Marketing experiences—even *virtual marketing experiences*—do not occur in a vacuum. They take place in the real world and the universe, against an economic, political, social, and cultural backdrop. Sometimes they set things in motion, sometimes dramatically alter the environment, but always sense, react, and reflect the mood and spirit of the moment, life, and the market.

A year-long marketing plan makes good business sense for budgeting purposes and a three-year or five-year plan sends a confident message to investors, supporters, and the public at large that the marketer is serious, knows where the company or organization wants to go, and has its strategy all mapped out. But in order to engage the consumer, marketers must be aware of the most current concerns—even as the current status may be shifting—regarding what is important to the target public.

Constantly updated statistics and round-the-clock breaking news, however, have created a cloud cover that threatens the best laid plans with sudden possibilities of dampness, severe storms, or perhaps bolts of lightning before a glimpse of sunshine might again be expected.

Change has always been a welcome fact of marketing life—and a very *costly* fact as well—as changes in society around the world occur with dizzying speed. Both short-term and longer-term planning become especially challenging, as plans must include an ability to adapt to shifts in societal and market trends, while still remaining competitive and focused on objectives.

Change is what helps fuel the hunger for *the next new thing* that will bring comfort, satisfaction, pleasure, happiness, and solutions to problems as well as success, relief from stress, and perhaps an escape from the everyday grind.

In developing marketing programs, there are occasions when even bad news can be a good thing. Businesses and organizations in the past have found that sometimes the most extreme crisis situations can present opportunities. Many marketers take the old saying, *when life gives you lemons, make lemonade* very seriously. Some people simply refuse to accept failure or defeat. It might seem naïve or unrealistic, but it works for them.

Timely research—getting a real-time sense of the market—is essential for companies or organizations when things are not going according to plan. Listening skills are more important than ever. Turning a business crisis to an advantage, not just surviving it, requires a good grasp of the facts at hand.

Sales and marketing strategist David W. Richardson advises, "Plan your presentation objective around the end result of listener acceptance."[1] Instead of only focusing on the form and substance of the message that will be presented, consider what in that message will be what people will most likely remember—and how they will use that information.

Brands, Experiences, Everyday Life, and Choices

It seems the order of the day for marketers is to aim for the most exciting, sizzling, entertaining, boldest, busiest, possibly loudest approach to snagging the attention of the public. When that approach is truly creative and proves effective marketing is credited with having done its job. Sometimes, however, it just ends up being bold, busy, and loud. At such times it is advisable to review what exactly motivates and convinces people to make the choices they do. Often, in one's zeal to break new creative barriers, the obvious is overlooked or ignored.

Familiarity makes people comfortable. Whether it is a familiar face, a city or town, a restaurant, accessories, family or friends—people tend to feel more at ease, safe, and confident around people and things they know. The challenge of engaging the public in a marketing effort is far less complex—and the effort's chances of succeeding become greater—when the connection can be created within a familiar context. Don't ever rule out the bold, exciting, or even the loud approach. But remember that in offering something unknown or daring, the boldly outside the norm may be overshadowed by its potential risk or fear factor.

In theory, people welcome—and respond very favorably—to products, ideas and experiences that are fresh, new, interesting and, under the right circumstances, exciting. Yet, such introductions are received less guardedly when they include or reflect elements of what is already known or within a particular consumer type's comfort zone.

Everything a person sees and hears is internally processed and weighed against what is already known. Every inclination and belief is used to measure the validity and value of new information received. A response might be an affirmation or agreement, a surge of interest and desire to know more, a laugh or smile, anger or outrage, indifference or dismissal.

Who is communicating can be as significant as *what* is being communicated. Word-of-mouth recommendations from friends, family, or professional colleague rank high in credibility and integrity. Celebrities are chosen for endorsements and as product spokespersons, in no small part, because the public not only recognizes the celebrities, but feels it *knows* these people.

When the stars of the long-running comedy shows *Friends* or *Will & Grace* appear in 15-second public service television spots, not as their TV characters, but speaking directly to the viewing audience, the strength of their participation is in the fact that people feel they know these actors. The audience is not supposed to feel the message is being pitched by someone famous, but by someone trusted and familiar. A connection is presumed to exist, despite the barrier of the television screen.

The vast majority of people in the world never attend (or even visit) Harvard, Yale, or Princeton, but know of their existence and prestige from years of media references, biographical notes, and because of often prominent people's associations with the universities as preeminent institutions of higher learning. The sense of familiarity and high opinion of the universities comes through the experiences of others, even people with whom no personal relationship exists.

Marketers understand that people make value judgments every day. Seeing the Harvard name on any of several business publications or on the spine of a book, for example, can attach a certain level of quality to the product, based on nothing other than the reputation of the school—whose faculty and administration doubtless had little or nothing to do with the magazines or books under consideration. People's predisposition to attach a value to the products is based on what they believe to be true about Harvard and the connection felt toward those identified with it.

Someone who perceives Harvard to be a prestigious institute of higher learning takes a certain "rub-off" experience in just owning the publication—call it a sense of "intelligence by association."

Another person sees or hears the word "Harvard" and immediately has an image of a "pointy-headed, elitist, liberal intellectual." It might be assumed that someone who connects that imagery and context to the name will *not* attach high or positive standards to products seeking to capitalize on it as a "brand" value and will not only *not* buy the products, but will leave them behind with a dismissive wave. Visitors buying products bearing the Harvard imprint (sweatshirts, T-shirts, jackets, coffee mugs, beer mugs, pens, etc.,) do so in part based on how they consciously or unconsciously relate its image and reputation to their own status and professional standing.

A terrific book by a fine author might rate a disdainful sniff from a person who notices the publisher has the same name as a place associated with a philosophy he or she does not like. The experience was only a mental exercise in association, but it determined whether or not a purchase decision was made. The principle involved is the same as rejecting a product on a store shelf because the product contains an ingredient with which the purchaser has had a negative experience.

Along with an uncertain economy, war and the

threat of terrorism, high unemployment and massive credit card debt, these prejudices and predispositions as they relate to the experiences of individuals with brands and reputations are what marketers are up against.

The examples emphasize again the importance of research, of knowing what those in the market like and dislike, and of *listening* to what the voice of the market is saying. It also helps to keep in mind that the marketer and the target market may hold widely different views and beliefs, which are subject to change. These beliefs don't have to be true or accurate, they just have to be real in the minds of those who hold them.

Ongoing Programs and the Status Experience

Ongoing marketing experiences—promotions designed to attract consumers and keep them coming back on a regular or sustained basis (versus just to take advantage of a one-time special offer)—are not new. Here are ten of the most consistently effective programs that can be adopted and/or *adapted* to fit virtually any company or organization, small or large, local or global:

- Airline mileage clubs allow travelers to accumulate points (or "miles") that can then be used for flight upgrades or free trips.

- Restaurants issue frequent-diner cards to patrons who receive a free meal after a specific number of meals have been purchased.

- "Members-only" discount plans from retailers charge an annual fee for the "privilege" of shopping in a store not open to the "general public"—even though rules for membership are virtually non-existent.

- Businesses initiate repeat-purchase programs that accumulate points redeemable for free bagels, yogurt, doughnuts, meals, merchandise, cash back, and a myriad of other premiums.

- More than a half-century ago (and right up to the present) merchants were offering S&H Green Stamps, Plaid Stamps, Blue Chip Stamps, Raleigh coupons, Camel Cash, and a myriad of variations on the concept to promote shopping at one establishment over another or to favor one brand over another, and the accumulated books of stamps or coupons could be redeemed for catalog merchandise.

- Free food buffets lure people into bars during "happy hour," the allocated period after the workday ended and before the dinner hour began.

- Hotel chains such as Hilton and Marriott

offer plans where guests earn free trips, car rentals, and lodging for accumulating paid nights at their various properties.

- "Bounce-back" cards are presented to customers and offer special discounts on future purchases.

- Restaurants offer "early-bird specials" in the form of reduced prices to senior citizens who dine earlier than the normal dinner rush.

- Many supermarkets designate one day each week for senior citizens, when prices are discounted and assistance is provided to shoppers.

Probably more people than not would say they consider supposed VIP status anywhere between silly and snobbish. Research, however, tells another story.

A *Wall Street Journal* report in 2004 noted the role status plays in creating a marketing experience. To some people, it might be enough just to be accepted as a "member," but to others, a capital "M" is a requirement. "You don't have to be very important these days to be a VIP. From symphonies to museums to rock concerts, America's entertainment, travel, and fitness industries are selling specialness—to everybody," the report noted.[2]

But ten of the promotional programs the *Journal*

identified are clearly *not for everyone.* Among the more upscale marketing experiences once considered to be exclusive perks of board members, trustees, and only the rich or famous, these can now be purchased by anyone over the counter or online—if the family budget or corporate expense account can handle it:

- Prime seating at a major movie studio premiere plus an escort to accompany the purchaser to a VIP after-film party to mingle with stars and entertainment industry executives (cost: $250 per person).

- Beyond the price of admission, a VIP tour pass can be purchased that allows visitors to bypass waiting lines and have "exclusive access to select backstage areas" at Universal Studio theme park in Orlando, Florida.

- For an annual fee of $295, "Members" receive two passes for United Airline's Red Carpet Club, a bottle of wine, and a free companion ticket every time the Member buys a full-fare ticket on a domestic flight.

- The Los Angeles Philharmonic orchestra offers an "Overture" membership at $250 per year that includes a private reception with the orchestra's conductor, cocktail parties, and backstage tours of the concert hall.

- Walk-on roles at the Orlando-UCF Shakespeare Festival are for sale.

- Billion Dollar Babes is an operation that runs a clothing-sample sale in New York and Los Angeles, where a $200 Platinum "Membership" means early admission and a separate dressing room.

- Special VIP packages for concert-goers include front-row seats, backstage passes, "premier" parking, and access through a private entrance.

- The Rock and Roll Hall of Fame offers a 90-minute private tour by the museum curator of a closed-to-the-public vault that includes "hidden treasures" of rock and roll, such as a Bob Marley dreadlock and blues legend Muddy Waters's passport.

- In New York, the Equinox is a health club with an "inner circle" Membership that permits access to a workout area with leather-upholstered weightlifting equipment and a lounge with a giant flat-screen TV, for an annual fee of $24,500.

- VIP donors to the New Jersey Performing Arts Center have the use of a private salon, where they and a few friends are served finger sandwiches and crab dip before viewing a performance of productions such as *The Full Monty* then later served chocolate-covered strawberries at intermission.

From the most simple, inexpensive, and understated effort to the high-end "premium" level program for the truly status conscious, an ongoing marketing experience can support plans aimed at building brand equity and brand loyalty, increasing visibility, and establishing a marketing position.

Presenting someone a T-shirt bearing a store logo is a promotion; but including a "Preferred Customer Membership Card" that provides discounts, admission to private sales, or perhaps nothing more than being added to the store's mailing list, can be a marketing experience that may have a long-term effect on the merchandiser's relationship with the customer.

Summary

- Attracting the public by creating a physical and emotional connection to a subject, once the province of creative directors, is now partly everyone's job.
- People of certain demographic groups are thought to be generally smarter, more aware or sophisticated, and perhaps also more

skeptical of many overused advertising techniques and claims.

- The climate created by unusual or well-publicized radical methods of creating awareness and attracting business encourages some marketers to take risks in reaching an increasingly jaded public.

- Creating a marketing experience that resonates cannot be a hit-and-run matter, as much of the public continues to require something be not just good, but also *fresh* and *sustaining*.

- The possibilities allow for one campaign to continue as another is tested or rolled out, as long as a cohesive message is maintained so the public will not be confused by competing campaigns.

- It is possible for a campaign to include a single marketing experience event and an interactive experience, as well as an ongoing program that sustains loyalty and builds equity while keeping the public and the subject together.

- A plan should reach the target market on an emotional, psychological, or sensory level *and* make certain to include a "value statement" in the marketing message.

- Involve participants on as many levels as possible. Being exclusionary can work against a marketer at different times. Someone entering a program at one level might move up to another if he or she has a good opinion of the subject.

- Marketing experiences do not occur in a vacuum, but take place in the real world against an economic, political, social, and cultural backdrop that sometimes dramatically alters the environment and the mood of the moment and the market.

- Familiarity makes people comfortable. The challenge of engaging the public and the chances of succeeding are greater when a connection is created within a familiar context.

- An ongoing marketing experience can help build brand equity, loyalty, and a strong marketing position.

Notes

1. The quotation attributed to David W. Richardson appeared in "Design Backwards" (Sales and Marketing Excellence, November 2003).

2. Quotation from "Well, Aren't You Special" by Paula Szuchman, *Wall Street Journal,* May 14, 2004.

Making the Marketing Experience Work

When Not Everyone WANTS to Have a Marketing Experience

Being confident of the value of the product, service, or subject of a marketing effort is good—some would say it is even *necessary* to do the job well. To be enthusiastic about it is even better. Yet, it is helpful to know that many or most of the people who make up the targeted market of the effort do not inherently share this enthusiasm, nor should it be assumed they would be receptive to the campaign or its message. In fact, years of market research has indicated the opposite to be the case: that the public largely believes there is too much advertising and hype, and people resent the intrusion and avalanche of clutter from junk mail, print ads, billboards, TV commercials, and spam—particularly pop-up ads that are referred to almost exclusively as *annoying.*

Still, marketers understand their job is to generate awareness and interest for products, services, companies, or other subjects, and to do so as if the public is eagerly awaiting the news—even if they know an audience is consciously resisting *listening* to them. The landscape is crowded with people competing for attention.

So to the greatest extent possible, marketers try to brightly package, direct, and *personalize* their messages. The public is well aware that bulk mailings are machine-generated by the millions of pieces, whether imprinted with individual names acquired through list brokers or internal databases, and that in the words "something special for you inside," the word "you" is actually referring to millions of still unknown people. Yet, a marketing plan should still seek to employ whatever devices are available that allow individual recipients of mail or viewers of ads to feel in some way linked personally to the subject.

All this is done in promoting products, styles, and trends with the hope that it will have the widest possible appeal to the masses. *And* this personal connection must be taken seriously as it will be reinforced—for better or worse—each time the product is seen, heard, mentioned, or used by the consumer.

In the 21st century, a time of rampant public cynicism, skepticism, and high-tech sophistication, it almost seems the entire premise is absurd—that people today are smart enough not to be influenced or moved by "we care about you" statements directed to a general and vast audience. The effort, it would seem, might be doomed simply for stretching the limits of credibility.

The public is indeed aware that *personal* letters going to millions of people all include the identical "exclusive" or "limited" offer, and that when a TV announcer says "you can count on us," he or she is speaking in the second person to an infinite number of people, not just to the person the term "you" might typically imply. For decades there has been an overuse of the strategic imperatives "look straight into the camera," "speak directly to the audience as if it were just one person," and "believe that direct marketing is giving you direct contact with each individual in the marketplace, if only as a whole." To describe the approach as illogical seems an understatement.

Marketing communication indeed is a tricky process in which logic and contradiction intersect on a regular basis and yet it somehow ultimately seems to make sense.

Consider the aspect of human nature in which nobody wants to be just one of the crowd, though instinctively every person wants to feel that he or she belongs or is an accepted part of a group or member of an audience. Even those who stand alone in the spotlight spend time on the other side of the microphone or lectern as well. From school desks and bleachers to front-row seats and boardroom tables, everyone has at some time been on the receiving end of presentations and performances, and can understand how being listened to and feeling accepted is important.

While wanting to feel unique or special, people will stand in line for hours waiting to buy one ticket for an event so that while sitting or standing among tens of thousands of other people, they could boast "they were there." It is the uniquely human quality of being able to feel special and personally connected— even as one member of a huge crowd.

Still, when someone steps up and asks, "Are you ready to hear about something good?," while no one expects the response to be *"no,"* it happens. Presentation, context, and timing have a great deal to do with whether or not the marketing magic works.

That not everyone will always be inclined to hear what someone else has to say seems as if it should be obvious. Marketers know this to be true, learning the lesson by having excellent, expensive ads and promotions misfire simply because something else occurred at the same time and diminished the impression or impact of the effort.

Some sales reps insist that *everyone* is a prospect for whatever they are selling, believing that such expressions of confidence have an empowering effect, but privately knowing that is not always the case. So the target market indicating it would be *receptive* to the message and would *accept it* is important, along with the *presentation*, *context*, and *timing* of what is offered.

A number of comedians are known for beginning their acts with old and intentionally bad jokes. When the audience groans, they will nervously tug at their collars and mutter, "Geeez, tough crowd."

The audience expects the line and laughs at what seems to be the comedian's discomfort, although it's part of the act and the audience knows it. But some people really *do* go to theaters and comedy clubs, sitting for hours with their arms folded across their chests, acting unbelievably bored and mumbling, "I don't think that's funny" after every comic bit. They go out determined *not* to laugh or be entertained—seeming to *dare* performers to entertain them. Maybe they don't want to be there or they are not feeling well. Perhaps they believe that their lives are falling apart. Whatever the story, these people are not out to have a good time or to put aside their problems for a while—*or are they?*

Why would anyone attend an entertainment event and summon all of his or her energy to resist being entertained? Maybe it is for the reasons suggested—or *maybe these people just enjoy being a "tough crowd."*

Some people genuinely enjoy having the reputation of being a "tough boss" or a "tough customer." They relish the experience of challenging someone to amuse or impress them and take pride in declaring, "I'm not easily impressed," "It really takes a lot to entertain me," "There is no way this guy will make me laugh." In more common everyday situations that relate to the subject of marketing they assert, "This guy thinks he's going to sell me something, but that's not going to happen."

That's *their* act. It can be hard on a comedian, and no less hard on the sales or marketing executive whose job or career can depend on generating a positive response. In reflecting on the cynicism of the times, it is common for people to say, *everybody is always selling something—usually it's themselves.*

Perhaps, but even if it's true that everyone is

selling that doesn't guarantee that everyone is, at that moment, in the mood to buy. Different people are moved by different motivating factors at different times. For many children and adults, the circus is truly *The Greatest Show on Earth*, but to others it is just another big, noisy, messy operation, distinguished by the aroma of elephant dung.

So it is now clear that while people may often view the same scenes very differently, to create an effective marketing experience requires that members of the target market be: (1) receptive to the message, (2) willing to accept it, and (3) impressed with its presentation. The message must also be set in the proper context and properly timed.

A marketing program can be brilliant, creative, innovative, and dazzling, but still there will be people who refuse to let their true feelings about it become known, particularly if those feelings are positive. They insist on summoning all their resistance to appear not even a little impressed. This aspect of human nature is not for marketers to explain, but it is important that marketers *be aware that it exists.*

If a certain segment of the public is steadfastly determined to resist, rebuff, or reject a marketer's efforts, perseverance alone will not likely overcome such feeling. But perhaps *knowledge* will.

Someone might not want to laugh or to buy anything or to be entertained at the particular time the message is first presented, but it is reasonable to believe that such a person could be responsive to *something* at *some time*. A marketer's task (and challenge) is to find the method—and the *time and context*—to connect with those who make up a perhaps highly diverse target market and to provide information, products, and services, sometimes even if people might not realize they want or need what is being offered.

Consider how often people say, whether shopping for themselves or for someone else or as a special occasion draws closer, "I haven't a clue what to get" or "I don't know which would be the best choice." Is a marketer in such situations forcing unwanted merchandise on the public or is he or she performing a valuable service?

This is not a situation where some cocky salesman brags about being able to sell refrigerators to Eskimos or is deceiving people into buying useless merchandise they do not want or need; this is about positioning and presenting products and services in their best light and at the same time *being responsive* to the needs and wants of the public.

For professional marketers, creating a perceived need or desire is not some slick maneuver; rather it's about watching, listening, planning and doing the job right. It is about knowing the market. Check the most current available research data on the target market to determine:

- What people are buying and doing in large numbers.
- What people want.
- What people expect.
- What they strongly *dislike.*
- What is the minimum standard they are likely willing to accept.
- What is the comfort zone of those who comprise the target market.
- What are the most frequently heard objections from the public or critics.
- What opportunities exist to address, neutralize, and overcome resistance.
- What are the best media or other vehicles for reaching the target market in a favorable environment.
- What is the best way to achieve the desired objective.

Ten points are listed and all begin with the word "what," yet none is a question. All must be statements of facts that provide essential information necessary to draft a well-focused plan.

The Main Event: A Memorable Marketing Experience

Establishing a *connection* between the marketer's product or subject and the consumer is a far more effective approach to marketing than mounting a costly saturation ad campaign in which the marketer puts out information that appears to be everywhere—TV, radio, billboards, mailings, Internet banners on hundred of high traffic web sites, point-of sale displays—all in the hope that someone notices. But viewing an ad or receiving a free T-shirt bearing a product name or a company logo or having a pop-up appear on a PC screen is *not* creating a marketing experience. Establishing an interactive exchange in which a consumer feels physically or emotionally involved or connected with a product or subject on some level *is* a marketing experience.

As with web sites that only have value when people are made aware of them, log on to them, and view or sample whatever information is made available to them, even the most dramatic and engaging marketing campaign will result in failure if no one knows about it. The subject of the effort is still a product, service, organization, cause, issue—something that must still be publicized and promoted to gain awareness before any type of experience can take place. To bring all energy and resources to bear on the "experience" aspect of the program alone falls short of the goal if the "marketing" part is given secondary (or lesser) consideration.

Companies and organizations invest millions of dollars to create an "Internet presence"—which basically has meant building a good web site that offers something the market wants. But it sometimes takes awhile for businesses to realize a wholly separate effort is required to make people *aware* these web sites exist and direct traffic to them.

If a marketer has something of value, it's a safe bet that people who want it enough will make the effort to find it, whether through a catalog, a web site, a telephone book, or a walk around the mall. But the number of people who can be counted on to put forth such an effort *unprompted* will likely not be significant enough to generate a sufficient profit to keep going, much less to dominate a category. It is up to the marketer to get the story out, create awareness and interest, and not simply expect it to be found by people who may or may not have reasons to go looking. A major element in effective marketing involves going where the market is.

A key aspect of the marketing experience is connecting with people on their own terms—particularly those who have shown resistance to traditional forms of advertising and promotion. It is also important that in the process of going where the market is, not to step on people along the way. Getting the message across to the right audience is essential, but in communicating with that specific audience be aware of the possibilities of annoying or offending either members of the targeted market group or those who are currently *not* part of that group. It is likely that some people who are not part of the target market may still have some influence with those who are. While focusing on being creative, aggressive, and confident, it is wise not to make enemies through simple thoughtlessness.

Even when ads are only minimally intrusive, they are *still* ads. After years of being bombarded and often overwhelmed by advertising, much of the public's "filtering mechanisms" kick in and the messages get tuned out. Additionally damaging to the cause is the fact that many ads presented through virtually all media can be not only *intrusive*, but are at times *abrasive and offensive.* It is as if the advertiser, in trying to "convey an attitude" that would cause people to stop and take notice, acted in such a way as to provoke the opposite action.

In an earlier example of a *Playboy* magazine campaign from decades ago ("What kind of man reads *Playboy?*"), the venue was carefully chosen. A pitch for subscribers was placed inside the magazine itself, and positioned in advertising and marketing trade media where people who care about the magazine would be. The art and copy reflected an insider's understanding of the tastes and preferences of the target audience. Two generations later *Playboy* continues to fine-tune its positioning, trying to attract new and younger subscribers while retaining older, long-time readers.

Remaining true to its core premise, the men's magazine recognizes that the marketplace has evolved. The company attempts to reach different demographic market segments using different media and messages (direct mail promoting a more sophisticated tone and discounts to older readers and past subscribers, while cross-selling merchandise that carries the brand's name; hotter ads are run on cable TV and the Internet, aimed at younger market segments; events and special interest media for special products—a wide variety of branded merchandise that appeals to still narrower market segments).

Identifying, understanding, and targeting the right market for the subject of the marketing effort is critical, but it is also important to position the subject correctly with *secondary* market segments. Marketing campaigns that exclude certain segments of the public by positioning the subject as being *only* appropriate for a particular group, inferring that the target group is more desirable than others, commit a marketing blunder. It says outsiders need not apply—a message that most assuredly will backfire at the subject's expense at some point in the future, if not sooner, then later.

Secondary markets can receive *less* attention in the marketing plan, but should be considered for what they might add and, in any case, should not be ignored or alienated.

Marketers trying to reach younger demographic segments have increasingly "edgy" campaigns with an *attitude* in an attempt to connect with them on their own youthful level. This too is almost always a mistake. The young target groups often view these efforts as patronizing and condescending ploys written and produced by a bunch of old guys who think this is how young people think and act. Timely market research is essential; opinions of management should be listened to, but not confused with the reality of what the research shows.

Again, not everyone responds to the same approach at the same time—or every time—and the importance of regularly taking the pulse of the market and listening to the public cannot be stressed enough.

To reach out and connect with consumers does not always require a blockbuster breakthrough idea and a campaign launched with great fanfare on a national or international scale (although those are very nice to experience at least once in a marketing lifetime). It can be a small, simple, low-tech approach, rolled out in test markets one at a time. The right approach is not necessarily the hot new idea with the most speakers; the right approach is *the one that works*.

The marketing experience can be packaged and presented as entertainment, an event, a challenge, a reward, a free gift, or any number of other familiar, yet effective, forms. In a perfect world the experience would be perceived as highly original and would be fascinating as well as successful. But on a slow, rainy day when everyone in the marketing department is tired, look for an interesting or new twist on the off-the-shelf ideas no one owns, such as:

- Product sampling.
- Free trial membership.
- Wine tasting.
- A "bake-off" or other such competition that invites people to demonstrate talent or share favorite foods, original recipes, specialties, or ideas using particular products or brands.
- An on-site special program at the home, school, town, or other designated location of a chosen recipient.
- Participation in an online discussion, election, or event.
- A competitive yet good-natured semi-literary event, such as Harry's American Bar & Grill's Annual "Bad Hemingway" writing contest.

- A scavenger hunt or collect-all-the-pieces-of-a-puzzle type of program.

These activities create an interaction—an experience—between a consumer and a brand, product, an organization, or other particular subject. Some of them are far from new, but they still deliver results. Each is a formula approach, yet each also falls outside of the usual contest or sweepstakes concept in that:

1. They all directly involve the consumer/participant in an activity that goes beyond simply filling out an entry form.

2. The sponsor's presence is ongoing and blatantly obvious, yet the public's (as well as the participants') resistance or objection to the brand's name or logo placement is non-existent or minimal when compared to negative reactions to even a 15-second commercial or 30-second sales pitch.

A Store and Something More

Historically, most consumers regard a visit to a store as . . . well, a visit to a store. Sometimes it is to purchase needed items, to get ideas, or just to pass the time. But companies and organizations staffed by people who are continually striving for the best and the brightest approaches to marketing manage to make each customer's visit to a store an event or, in keeping with the subject of this book, an *experience*.

New York's once-legendary F.A.O. Schwartz, for example, made every child's trip to the mid-town toy store any day of the year seem like the brightest of holidays—like a visit to Santa's workshop. Yet, for decades the extremely successful retailer remained in a class by itself. Today, for numerous reasons, the F.A.O. Schwartz stores that had grown to become a thriving upscale national chain have closed and the reconfigured organization maintains only flagship locations in New York and Las Vegas, continuing to serve other markets through wholly separate and distinct Internet and catalog operations.

But for decades F.A.O. Schwartz was considered special among retailers. People halfway around the world knew of its existence and its reputation as a child's fantasy world of toys.

The hit motion picture *Big* includes a classic scene that takes place inside the store, in which two of the movie's stars, Tom Hanks and Robert Loggia, make music by dancing on a giant piano keyboard. A crowd of delighted shoppers surrounds the characters, cheering them on. Moviegoers by the millions connect with the film, seeming to get close enough to feel as if they are part of the crowd, swept up in the music and the moment. For years after the film's release, people sought out the giant keyboards at F.A.O. Schwartz stores, repeating the scene with their own family members and friends assuming the stars' roles.

As such memorable scenes were being played out with the whole world watching, other stores went along perpetuating the old system of aisles and shelves/buyers and seller, showing little or no effort to emerge and engage the public in enjoyable or unique personal shopping experiences.

What made this odd in marketing terms was it was well known that a variety of relatively simple, cost-effective alternatives existed to the traditional system. Most businesses and organizations simply lacked either the imagination or energy to make the leap from the old ways to try something different.

Pizza shops and candy makers, for example (and virtually any company or business that turns itself "inside-out" just by putting its kitchen or workshop in its street-level window), invariably attracts crowds of onlookers admiring the "artists at their work." By showing the public how its products are created or demonstrating its skills, the storeowners encourage fascinated passersby to pause, gather, enjoy, and spread the word about the interesting businesses that virtually present live shows in their windows everyday, without doing anything but going about their normal routines.

Seeing a pizza chef throw a ball of dough into the

air, spinning it, and turning it into a round, flat pie is to an onlooker as entertaining as the mimes, magicians, and sidewalk performers of another era. Candy makers, ice cream shops, baby photographers, portrait artists, barbers, stylists, and others who allow the public a glimpse inside their private worlds and workspaces are equally as entertaining to watch. Of course it helps to "dress" the business in such a way as to let people on the outside know the interior is pleasant, friendly, and welcoming.

Like restaurants with singing waiters and street vendors that tell jokes and perform tricks, getting a bit of entertainment with the merchandise at no additional cost, or being offered an opportunity to step inside, relax, and be treated as if something special is going on, typically makes people feel better about a place and brings them back again and again not just to shop, but to share the experience.

Some of the more clever and appealing, though not cost-prohibitive, approaches that engage consumers are based on simple principles of a well run business or organization: do something well, enjoy it, create a positive atmosphere, and share that on some level with the visiting public.

A cooking demonstration in a department store or a supermarket, for example, is an idea that dates back a very long way, yet continues to attract people who become fascinated with something that would not normally seem to entertain them. Cooking an omelet at home is not exactly considered a form of high art, but the same omelet being prepared in the center of a department store draws crowds, applause, and smiles—and sends people home with a story to tell, a recipe or two, and (when managed properly) a new frying pan.

Visual presentations or theatrics seem well suited to restaurants, stage shows, toy stores, and sidewalk vendors, but could such an approach work for other less lively, glamorous, or "visual" enterprises?

How, for example, does a marketer create a marketing experience for a subject that doesn't seem to lend itself to activities typically considered entertaining, or even interesting, much less easy to understand? Consider what might go into creating a marketing experience for a:

- Technology company.
- Financial services organization.
- Purveyor of cleaning supplies.
- Law firm.
- Insurance agency.
- Drug store.
- Hospital.
- Village or city.

- Any of a myriad of other companies, businesses, institutions, causes, or issues.

Connecting with the public, engaging people, holding their interest, and closing the deal takes planning and action to bring a subject to the public's attention and to move the public to respond. The process includes:

- Conducting and managing current research—learning all that can be known about the target market segment.

- Identifying what makes a subject unique, distinctive, or sets it apart from others in its field—in marketing terms, finding the *unique selling proposition*—not simply believing it is enough to claim being the "best" or the "largest" or the "oldest" in the business.

- Taking the pulse of the market to determine the public's tastes, wants, needs, concerns, tolerance levels, and checking the "hot buttons."

- Understanding that being the oldest or largest will likely mean little or nothing to the public, but that such claims leave an individual or organization vulnerable to demands that such statements be validated by an objective authority.

- Looking and listening to what competitors are doing now, have done in the past, or what those in other fields are doing successfully that might be adapted or applied to other products, industries, companies, areas, or causes.
- Creating a marketing plan.
- Making a commitment to succeed.

The case studies section of this book examines various approaches companies and organizations have employed, but consider some of the stores that were *not* primarily retailers and, as such, did not have the benefit of typical high visibility brand advertising or co-op funding. Their aim was in part to position their own private label products, while offering experiences unique by their presence in the retail marketplace. Consider, for example,

- The Disney Store
- The American Girl store
- The Ralph Lauren Polo store
- IKEA
- NikeTown

- The Sony store

- The Body Shop

- The Discovery Channel store

- Starbucks

- Krispy Kreme Doughnut shops

These establishments:

1. All operate in or around "average looking" and accessible store retail locations.

2. Do not regard themselves to be first a *store,* but rather specialists or experts in a particular field.

3. All offer a unique setting or atmosphere and invite an interaction between consumers and products beyond just looking at displays.

4. All offer their own private brand of merchandise.

5. Each strives to provide visitors and customers with a memorable experience, rather than just a trip to a store.

Many factors influence and define the specific focus of the experience to be created:

- *The objective of the effort*—What is to be accomplished?

- *The market to be addressed*—What is its size and demographic profile?

- *The product, organization, subject, or industry*—Obviously, considerations involved in creating a marketing experience for introducing a new candy bar or soft drink will be significantly different from those focused on creating a marketing experience to promote an automobile, a swimming pool, a vacation resort, or a museum; just as engaging audiences in a fundraising effort to help homeless people would differ from efforts to benefit public television, provide money for medical research, or draw attention to a social issue.

- *Traditions*—Some types of experiences are more welcome and will have a positive pre-sell element or existing broad appeal, while others might be considered inappropriate under certain conditions for ethnic or religious reasons or due to the political or social climate.

- *Location*—The range of appropriate or most opportunistic options available in certain climates, communities, and cultures should be considered in terms of identifying alternatives from the safest to the boldest.

- *Timing*—Look for opportunities presented by the season, calendar-linked occasions, or relationships to certain events like back-to-school, graduation, winter holidays, spring break, June weddings, summer vacation, or some tie-in to a particular anniversary, commemoration, or special event (such as a centennial, world's fair, sports tournament, championship, etc.). Is it best to go with the precedent or attempt to create new occasions or traditions that better position attention of the subject?

- *Resources*—From facilities and available materials and people to the size of the budget, what a marketer can accomplish within a specific time frame will vary greatly depending on what he or she has to work with.

The marketing program, while it should be constructed around the product, service, or other subject—and be tuned-in to the climate of the market—can also reflect the personality and energy of the marketer or the marketing team.

Sometimes the best idea might be very conservative or even seem simplistic. In other cases, it can appear far-out, wild, or edgy.

Perhaps the plan involves reintroducing a program that was successful in past years, fell out of fashion, lost market share, and has been updated to combine elements of nostalgia with the competitive demands of current times and circumstances. To continue building on an idea that worked and continues to work, or has worked before under different market conditions, is not copping out, taking the easy route, or showing a lack of creativity or imagination. A good idea is a good idea, even if it may seem familiar or derivative and some members of the marketing or management team are becoming bored, restless, or simply want to make changes.

The effort should not be driven by ego or by the chance to win an award, but by what the voice of the market says the public wants, will embrace or appreciate, and what is most likely to succeed. If all the best ideas came from the same few geniuses, the same brands would always be the market leaders and awards programs would have no suspense. That doesn't happen. *Advertising Age* rarely names the same person its "Marketer of the Year" more than once and marketing chiefs at the best-run organizations never take being the category leader for granted.

Life's Own Marketing Experiences

Some marketers, fixated on developing the big idea, are not open to considering the possibilities that exist before their eyes. The result is that opportunities are missed.

Many bright, interesting, and successful marketing experiences are not initiated by marketers, but by life itself. Ideas that become the nucleus of big plans originate with news and events triggered or driven by members of virtually all segments of society and can easily go unnoticed.

The very concepts of originality, creativity, and innovation are often simply the results of someone seeing things in ways others have not seen them before.

If marketers are alert enough to recognize and seize opportunities when and where they arise, the potential to maximize marketing efforts are virtually limitless.

Consider the number of events, encounters, plans, ideas, suggestions, or daily activities that involve marketing on both conscious and unconscious levels. Most of the common occurrences of everyday life include identifiable links—choices, purchases, sales, and decisions—that are (or were) marketing-driven.

Begin with the act of waking up and a person's typical daily routine:

- The choice of a clock or radio (and the selection of a radio station or type of music or sound) that people use to wake up each morning.
- Whether to begin the day with a shower, a walk, or some type of exercise routine.
- What to wear, how to dress, what personal care products are involved—from soap, shampoo, hair products, and toothpaste to tissues, deodorant, antiperspirant, cologne, eyeglasses or contact lenses, and various accessories.
- The choice of whether or what to eat for breakfast, whether to take a vitamin or a prescription drug, and the selection of morning coffee, tea, milk, juice, or something else.
- Using a toaster, a blender, toaster oven, coffee maker, or microwave oven.
- The decision to buy or have delivered a newspaper, tune in to a radio station, or select a morning news or other television program.
- Whether to use public transportation, carpool, or drive a particular car for specific

reasons ranging from cost and comfort to environmental concerns or appropriateness to the situation.

- The circumstances under which people interact with other people throughout the day, evening, week, weekend . . .

Between waking up and reaching the door to the outside world, it is likely that a person will be exposed to somewhere between dozens and hundreds of products, logos, and brand packages.

Depending on how literally the term "the marketing experience" is applied—and whether the experience is exclusively visual, otherwise sensory, psychological, or emotional, or overtly interactive, such as choosing and using a certain type of shaver or toothbrush, robe, or towels; gym or workout clothes; exercise equipment or videos; visiting a health club, swimming pool, running track or exercise class; or using a Walkman or other music player, or a Palm Pilot. Whether the experience is pleasurable, functional, conscious, or unconscious, it normally involves one or more aspects of marketing.

Time out.

Taking a shower or brushing one's teeth is a marketing experience? How did that get sold to the CEO? Different people will attach differing interpretations.

A marketing experience does not need to be

constructed around roller coasters, flashing lights, or a marching band.

Few people might disagree that taking a new car for a test drive and being presented with its unique features would qualify as a marketing experience. It seems silly to think of the most routine acts in commercial terms. But consider how the first-time (or the ongoing) use of a six-setting massaging showerhead or a "sonic" toothbrush—where the user's eye or hand looks directly at or beyond the product's brand logo— is significantly different from test-driving a new car and, after buying it, reinforcing the product/consumer connection through repeated use in one's daily life. The distinction virtually doesn't exist.

If a person were asked to try an electric toothbrush at a store and did, that would be a marketing experience. The experience is repeated to greater and lesser degrees with continued use of the product.

It is also an example of how the marketing process does not end with the presentation of a product or service or even with its purchase and delivery, but reinforces or challenges the purchase decision again and again.

Every time a person uses a particular brand or product, a marketing *impression* is made. That impression may be positive, negative, or neutral, sometimes not triggering awareness of the connection until it reaches an extreme point on the *sensory satisfaction spectrum:*

- If a toaster overcooks a muffin, what might be a typical consumer reaction toward the product—and its manufacturer?
- If a hairdryer causes a fuse to blow or performs below expectations, how might its purchaser feel about the product or brand?
- If a precooked breakfast is pronounced incredibly delicious a moment after removing it from a microwave oven or a toaster oven—or if it appears uncooked, or the consumer burns the roof of his or her mouth, what is likely to follow?

In each case, the answer is *a strong expression of satisfaction or dissatisfaction with the product, the company that made it, the place of purchase, and just possibly every other branded entity associated with it.* The next step is a positive or negative remark about the company or product at a future time when it might come up in conversation or when someone asks for a product recommendation.

A product that does not perform as expected, or for the length of time expected, or proves disappointing to its purchaser or user creates a *negative* marketing experience that can have a ripple effect and lead to bad word-of-mouth advertising for a long time.

Certainly it is smarter marketing to pre-empt negative word-of-mouth or consumer disappointment by delivering what is promised and by not becoming so consumed in the dazzling marketing experience that the focus on the quality and value of the product or service is obscured. One should not be short-changed to benefit another.

A marketer must become acclimated to seeing the opportunities that exist all around for marketing and for creating marketing experiences in everyday life. In many situations the driving force for such experiences are consumers themselves as they focus on particular occurrences and activities. A big event that is totally unique is great when inspiration and circumstances collide. Until that moment, however, don't let the small and obvious possibilities go overlooked.

June, for example, is a great month for traditions . . . and for marketing. Think graduation, beginning of summer, and the virtual sweepstakes of marketing, the June wedding.

Clearly a wedding presents not only a special day for a couple, but a huge opportunity for marketers involved in a myriad of products and services, including (but not limited to) jewelry and stationery, clothing, travel planning, and gifts of every variety from the simple and practical to the wildly unusual, unique, and bizarre. Manufacturers and providers of products and services have a theme, an event link, an occasion, a party, a special moment in time, and an opportunity to relive it all again in a celebration timed to the same day year after year.

The act of dating presents no less of an opportunity to create, position, and wrap a virtually endless array of products, services, and events—at home and away—into something that takes on a special meaning and significance when it is now tied to a relationship, from meeting for a cup of coffee or a hamburger or pizza to a weekend getaway, new shoes, a wristwatch, or fragrance. A single flower, a carriage ride, a notepad, or a Coke has the potential to be the center-piece or the trigger of a romantic and meaningful mo-ment that can change lives. Begin looking for it.

Certain degrees and types of products and services come with a level of visibility and opportunity that are already part of consumer consciousness. These might include visits to shopping malls or automobile dealer-ships for *test-drives, promotions, demonstrations, performances, elaborate interactive exhibits, partici-pation games that include gifts or prizes . . .*

With that in mind, consider the marketing possibil-ities for products and services that relate to situations that are not typically viewed as marketing platforms, but hold creative seeds ready to be planted, such as:

- Parties
- Dating
- Vacations
- Coffee with friends
- Meeting for a drink
- Entertaining friends at home
- Business travel
- Motor trips
- Moving
- Home remodeling
- In-home entertaining
- Visits to museums, parks, beaches, or the zoo

The most commonly regarded "social experiences" create a platform for possible *marketing experiences*. When someone uses expressions such as, "let's do lunch" or "let's meet for a drink," is it important at that time to make a particular type of impression? Could it lead to something more—from a new friendship to romance or a possible business contact or a job offer? Simple social connections typically involve deciding:

- Where to meet to have the right type of setting, atmosphere, or mood.

- The appropriate clothing for the occasion and place.

- Whether or not the occasion requires or suggests the purchase of a new outfit, or a haircut or styling, or that a particular book be read first.

- If it is necessary to bring any items or arrange for accessories that will make the encounter go better (a briefcase, notepad and pen, flowers or a gift, a camera, photocopies of documents, cellular phone, a rental car, etc.).

Keep in mind that each person has a role to play. Not all people are consumers in every situation. A person in another profession might think that meeting for a drink or a lunch was about going somewhere to eat or drink or meet—and from that person's perspective, that might be all it is or needs to be.

But a marketer imagining someone meeting for a drink or a lunch—whether for business or social reasons—should identify what that someone might want or need to make the connection as good as it can be, and consider what possible opportunities such a situation might present for creating experiences.

A radio ad might plant an idea with a suggestion that, "Sometimes a special occasion demands a special kind of place" and offer images of a romantic setting, with the right atmosphere, wine, and music, or a business environment with quality, service, and décor designed to impress the most discriminating executive. A companion print ad in carefully chosen publications can expand on the imagery, offering privacy, unsurpassed service, and . . . something extra. (The "something extra" can be for the creative department to work out—perhaps private phones or Internet connections at the table, complimentary wine with dinner, special menu items . . . .)

The objective of the exercise is for the marketer to think of the social experience or business experience and examine the details of such a situation to determine possible opportunities to create a marketing experience.

Using the restaurant again as an example, is an ad for a restaurant a marketing experience? No.

Is a complimentary sampling of wines, cheeses, or other foods; a tableside fashion show; a personal photograph taken of guests; strolling musicians who take requests; or any such similar activity that involves the customer with the business a marketing experience? Yes.

Virtually all other listed situations—moving, in-home entertaining, motor trips, etc.—afford a variety of opportunities for marketers to place and show products and services with subtlety, allowing consumers to see, touch, smell, feel, and experience the subject in a welcoming context.

Again, the objective is to look *for* marketing experience opportunities in places and situations where previously one looked passed them. Look as well to what is applied marketing in common practice and develop ways to modify, adapt, or enhance the experience to other products, companies, businesses, or organizations. Think of:

- The beverage distributor that offers complemintary soft drinks on the beach (product sampling).

- A hotel that provides free limo service to nearby luxury shopping areas (an amenity at many fine hotels).

- The snack manufacturer that makes free samples of products available to riders in taxicabs and on airplanes (promotion).

- The outlet mall that pays the tolls for motorists who leave the highway at the mall's designated exit (goodwill device).

- Restaurants that offer an adult-supervised play area away from the dining room so parents can enjoy a meal without feeling guilty or neglectful of their small children.

- The genius of the Book-of-the-Month Club concept in which the *seller* picks the merchandise for the customer not just once in a while, but 12 to 15 times per year and by calling customers "members" qualifies them for discounts and additional special offers of "selected" merchandise. (Note that the concept led to "record clubs," which delivered CDs, tapes, videos, DVDs, *and* selected books, and later to the "Fruit-of-the-Month Club" and "coffee clubs," which essentially turned customers into subscribers as well as regular, exclusive consumers and users of the marketing organization's lines of products.)

This is a "starter list" of experience marketing ideas that might be adapted or inspire such applications by other businesses or organizations. There exists a wide range of possibilities between a free "membership" card issued by a retailer with discounts for "preferred customers" and the construction of an all-out theme park that encourages people to feel especially good about a product or company, regard the brand or company as its "provider of choice," and keep them coming back.

Creating the marketing experience challenges the creative capabilities of the marketer. It incorporates elements of brand marketing, affinity marketing, relationship marketing, and multi-level marketing concepts with customer service and event management concepts. Ideas that work evolve into new ideas or good ideas used in combination with other good ideas. The result can be a highly original and innovative approach. Consider the possibilities and expand the list.

Think of a person who has sat quietly in the dark and known a "religious" experience and now feels a new awareness.

The message to marketers is that when planning a marketing campaign:

- Know the market—and what matters most to those who comprise the market.
- Study research and begin with what is known, acceptable, and comfortable for the consumer.
- Stretch the limits of creativity.
- Accept the challenge and don't hold back.
- Give people what they *think* they want—*and* offer them a choice of trying something new that might be a departure for them,
- Prepare well, then trust your judgment.
- Feel good about what you are doing.

If the marketing experience is satisfying for those who conceive it, there is a greater likelihood of that being true for the public as well.

Summary

- Generate awareness and interest for a subject, even though much of the public believes there is already too much advertising and hype, and resents getting more junk mail, ads, Internet pop-ups, and spam.
- Because everyone is selling doesn't guarantee that everyone is in the mood to buy.
- Different people are moved by different motivating factors at different times.
- Creating a marketing experience requires both the marketer and the market be receptive to the message and its presentation, promise, and timing.
- Research data must determine what people want, are buying, and doing; what they expect, but are likely willing to accept; what they dislike; what will address, neutralize, and overcome resistance; and what media best reaches the target market.
- Connect with the public on its terms, especially people who dislike ads.

- An entertaining place makes people feel good and brings them back to shop and share the experience.

- Connect with the public, engage people, hold their interest, and close the deal with planning and actions.

- Conduct and manage research, identify what is unique, distinctive, or sets the subject apart from others.

- Take the market's pulse to determine public tastes, needs, concerns, tolerance levels, and hot buttons.

- Many marketing experiences are initiated by life, originating with news and events triggered or driven by all segments of society.

- Factors that influence and define the experience to be created include the objective of the effort; the market to be addressed; the product, organization, subject, or industry; traditions, location, timing, and resources available to support the program.

- Know what matters most to the people and allow the strategy and tactics to reflect what the public feels is known, acceptable, and comfortable.

- Stretch creatively and don't hold back.

- Give people what they *think* they want—*and* offer them a choice of something new and different.

- Prepare well, trust your judgment, and feel good about what you are doing.

Interpreting The Marketing Experience and Taking a Closer Look

Introduction to Part Two

In the days when "American enterprise" was a term used to describe business, most business concentrated on only one item: The ice cream shop was the place to go for ice cream—which was usually made right in the store by its owners; the shoe store just sold shoes; the list of products available from the local blacksmith didn't take up too much space on the sign. The marketing experience was a far less complicated process.

Of course, over time, various enterprises became more "enterprising." The ice cream shop added a variety of candies and, later, sandwiches to its menu. The shoe store also began selling hosiery, handbags, gloves, and ultimately any additional accessories that fit on the shelves and could be in any way related to the core product. The marketing experience would shift into overdrive; so many products, so many messages, so little time . . .

Malls and department stores sold "the shopping experience" of the place itself, not putting particular emphasis on any one item, but seeking to make shopping at Saks Fifth Avenue, Neiman-Marcus, Sears, or Target an entertaining adventure in elegance, fun— sometimes in *speed.*

As marketers and their consumers became more sophisticated, the idea of *providing* or *doing something more* became as much a part of the process as the products of services involved.

Managers of hospitals realized no one had the exclusive franchise anymore—there was often more than one hospital in a mid-size town or village. People had choices about where to go for services. The same held true for doctors, lawyers, financial advisers, museums, vacation resorts, entire cities—even *countries*. Where would Las Vegas be without tourism?

Tourist destinations, museums, art galleries, national parks, branches of the military, and houses of worship, have all recognized—as have the seemingly endless list of product and services companies—the need to distinguish and differentiate themselves from others in their respective categories. As this section will show, some of them have done it quite well.

The word "experience" is one most adults understand without having it defined, but like many common words, people frequently attach their own interpretations to it. One of the most popular quotes in recent history is this response to a questioner: . . . *it depends on what your definition of the word 'is' is.*

According to the most recently published edition of the Oxford English Dictionary, as a *noun*, experience is (1) practical contact with and observation of facts or events; (2) knowledge or skill acquired over time; (3) an event or occurrence that leaves an impression on one; and, as a *verb*, it is to (1) encounter or undergo (an event or occurrence); or to (2) feel (an emotion).

As with the debate noted earlier about what qualifies in marketing terms as "experiential," the same reference source characterizes that word as "involving or based on experience and observation." It can be expected that the opposing camps will continue to argue that, the Oxford dictionary notwithstanding, those who "observe" should not be accorded quite the same status as those who more actively "engage" in an "experience." It seems a fair distinction.

Perhaps a dictionary should not be the final arbiter of what constitutes an experience or if, in effect, "observing" an experience that then triggers an emotion should be considered pretty much on the same level as the experience itself—just as long as emotion is a factor.

In marketing, the award typically goes to the winner. That is, if a marketing campaign achieves its objective and the consumer finds satisfaction as a result of exposure to the subject of that marketing campaign, then it could be argued the same principle as *"seeing is believing"* takes over. Essentially, to experience something is to *feel* some sense of a subject, whether that feeling has reached all the five senses or has only touched the mind or heart.

As with most approaches to marketing, no one way should be considered the *only* way.

In the next section of this book a variety of cases are examined. They range from dolls to doughnuts and high tech to shrimp, museums to gatherings of space alien enthusiasts. Some examples are elaborate while others are fairly basic. The reasons they were included—and placed in what might appear to be a "random order"—is to illustrate that a marketing experience, whether it is centered around meeting for a cup of coffee or being transported to a political convention floor nearly a half-century ago, can be as simple or complex as individual objectives and resources require.

Every successful enterprise began somewhere and each most likely aimed high, at least having aspirations to perhaps be "the next McDonald's" or "another Microsoft." Sometimes investment bankers provide millions in start-up capital and experts are brought in to fill every key post. Other times, a person might launch an idea from a basement, a garage or a room in his or her parents' home. There's virtually no staff. It is hoped that the millions of dollars will come later.

Using case studies as not just informational success stories but examples of inspiration and vision that might be adapted and applied to even unlikely products, services, or subjects, marketers are again asked the advertising question, "Can you see yourself in this picture?" In some instances the experience is envisioned as part of the initial strategy; or it can be "consumer-driven" and happen after-the-fact, possibly even led or inspired by an enterprising third party.

Visualize it; shape it; try it; and remember that sometimes a one-size-fits-all jacket looks very good with the sleeves rolled up.

Placing the Marketing Experience

Marketers typically take the position that the subject of a marketing effort, whether it is a bar of soap, a bar of candy, a bar and grill, or a bar association, should be regarded—and as such positioned—as a *brand*. And as a brand, the subject must then be differentiated from everything else within its industry and category, as well as from offerings in other categories and industries. Every successful brand is identified by basic core qualities or characteristics that contribute to shaping its image, and from those qualities and that image effective campaigns and programs can be developed.

The same premise holds true for places—resorts, shopping malls, office towers, cities, even for entire countries. As the subject of a marketing program, a place should be treated as a brand. The objective of the marketing effort for the subject place might be to attract meetings and conventions, new or relocated businesses, tourism, real estate development, events and festivals, factory construction, or new residents.

Clearly, tourism generates the major percentage of revenue for many locations and areas, and in some countries is even the basis of their national economies.

Having noted that *experience* can be both a noun and a verb, can we also then say that an experience can be a *place*?

Largely as a result of effective marketing, a particular reputation, image, or "attitude" becomes associated with a location and comes quickly to mind when people live or work in—or just visit or *think about*—such places as Hawaii, Jamaica, Paris, Beverly Hills, Las Vegas, Miami Beach, New York City, Detroit, or Washington, DC, to list only a few.

Virtually every place has something special upon which it can focus to distinguish itself—some characteristic that few or no others can claim, from a perfect climate, white beaches, being the birthplace of a president, great surfing, horse racing, redwood forests, or a Wild West museum to being the artichoke capital of the world.

Marketers understand the power of the correct location and the right address. Even some residents of the buildings could probably not provide the actual street address in New York for the United Nations Plaza or for Rockefeller Center. But except for mail and package deliveries, their street numbers and zip codes are unimportant to the public at large. Each location suggests its own particular image or impression and its name is worth a thousand mental pictures.

To visit, live, work, or shop at one of these locations is for many people an experience in itself. For millions of consumers each year, just *being there* for a visit or a brief stopover is enough to establish both a physical and a psychological connection that then registers as a sensory experience.

Usually, when managed well, that experience leads to memories and the acquiring of merchandise, property, memberships, or something that creates a *bonding* or *linking* relationship on some level between the person and the place that remains long after his or her departure.

The cases in this chapter examine places and their related unique products, services, companies, organizations, and institutions that all or in part are the marketing vehicles that position *places* as brands.

More than a few marketers use variations on the line, *"experience the thrill of being there"* to promote a myriad of events, concerts, golf courses, amusement parks, islands, thousands of tourist destinations, and beaches adjoining time-share condominiums. But is just "being there" enough to create either a *thrill* or an *experience,* much less both?

The answer is *sometimes.*

For some individuals, just approaching the hills outside of Salzburg in Austria—which people may recall "came alive" in the motion picture *The Sound of Music*—is a rich, breathtaking, overwhelming experience, as if stepping into a painted masterpiece that perhaps was not a scene that existed in reality. Others might shed a tear when standing within the shadow of France's Eiffel Tower, a site associated with history, romance, and much of what the city of Paris has come to embody. Still others regard the two sites as hills and a tower, and wonder what's the big deal? For them, neither the existence of the locations nor to physically connect with them constitutes a significant experience on any meaningful level.

People who are emotionally moved by seeing an ocean sunset or a baby sleeping are *experiencing* something special, and even if the scene is passive, serene, or still—and only they feel that emotion—it is nonetheless an experience.

The experience of participating in a church service reaches different people on vastly different levels.

For some, just *arriving* at major events or historic, beautiful, luxurious, romantic, or special locations—such as Carnegie Hall, the canals of Venice, the NASA Space Center, the White House, the Grand Canyon, or the harbor at Martha's Vineyard—is an experience in itself. In no small way, each of these destinations has been heavily marketed through the years to have the image and reputation that does indeed allow visitors to *"experience the thrill of being there."*

To capitalize on the uniqueness or importance of a location can take many forms—educating, informing, entertaining—and can be represented in story, song, film, fine oil paintings, comic books, snow globes, and key chains; a single, powerful presentation or the cumulative result of many diverse elements.

But before, after, and *while* experiencing being there, marketers for each location must examine the opportunities for positioning and promoting branded or related merchandise, providing services, generating revenue, and encouraging visitors and guests to return.

Nashville, Tennessee, also has a rich and unique history. The state's chosen nickname is "The Volunteer State," but mention Nashville to tens of millions of people around the world and their thoughts turn not to volunteers, but to country music.

For generations, long before sequin shirts and electric guitars added glitz and volume, there was the music exemplified by Hank Williams, Hank Locklin, Hank Snow, the Carter Family, women named Tammy, and families that sometime seemed to have more children because the act needed a fiddler or banjo picker. Country music was the town's business, its biggest export, its greatest attraction, and its lifeblood at the center of its daily routine as well as its economy.

Nashville—Music City USA: Experiencing the Location

Today Nashville calls itself "Music City USA" and its promoters are well aware that other markets would very much like to have a piece of the action that defines the public's love of country music as not so much a sound, a tradition, or an art form, but as a booming commercial enterprise.

Nashville remains the home base for most of country music's top stars in the United States. It is also the location of the Country Music Hall of Fame and the world famous Grand Ole Opry, the theater stage where legendary performers began their careers and continue to perform year after year. Tastes may change, but music lovers and other visitors still come to Nashville from all over the world.

It is not unusual for performers who are over 70 or 80 years old and long gone from the hit record charts to fill an auditorium with generations of loyal fans. While rockers and pop stars' careers might be tightly linked to the success of a single record album or CD, country music fans stay faithful to performers, requesting to hear songs that media archives abandoned years before.

Major music companies headquartered in New York and in Los Angeles record their country music acts in Nashville to achieve a sound that they insist does not seem natural or authentic when produced anywhere else.

Do performers really feel somehow different singing and playing their songs in Nashville? Is to perform or record there a special experience for the performers? Can fans tell the difference and hear a "Nashville sound" that doesn't come through on recording sessions that took place in another town? Why do the music companies make such a point of printing, "Recorded in Nashville" on the record albums, CD packaging, and promotional materials?

Fans, performers, producers, and the music companies all maintain that it *does* make a difference—that a unique *experience* takes place when recording a song in Nashville, a *feeling* that doesn't occur anywhere else. Without addressing the scientific or spiritual reasons why this may or may not be true, suffice to suggest that if country music fans and others connected with the form attach some special connotation to Nashville and support products made there, a marketer wanting to connect with that target audience had better know it.

Through the 1960s, the '70s, and beyond, a stroll down Nashville's "Music Row," the city's crowded enclave of recording studios, music publishing companies, talent agencies, and rehearsal halls, meant passing the:

- Barbara Mandrell Year-Round Christmas Store
- Crystal Gayle Gift Shop
- Conway Twitty Record Shop
- Ernest Tubb Record Store
- Randy Travis' Western Store
- Charlie Daniels Museum
- George Strait's Texan Connection Wax Museum

And there are countless other businesses that have been established to pay tribute to, and capitalize on, performers whose careers spanned decades and who now lend their names to restaurants and souvenir shops. The Everly Brothers' family business is a well-known guitar string operation and the late guitarist Chet Atkins is one of several Nashville music greats to have a street named in his honor.

Today, interspersed with local landmarks and silhouettes of cowboy hats, boots, and flattop guitars, are virtually every major hotel, motel, restaurant franchise, and national brand name establishment a consumer could want, from McDonald's to The Gap. Still, contemporary tastes notwithstanding, it is the link to the birth of country music and the names that define it that attract tourists and other consumers from around the world who want to feel they are standing, walking, eating, sleeping, or staying where someone who created the music that shaped their lives once traveled.

As with other marketing challenges, cities such as Nashville need first a plan with a:

- Clear objective
- Sharply identified unique selling points
- Defined strategy
- Tactics adopted to meet the objective

The country music connection has been emphasized over several prosperous decades. In many respects, Nashville might be a fine city with good schools, transportation, Sears, Target, Starbucks, multiplex theaters, Borders, and Barnes & Noble. But those are also the characteristics of many other cities in the United States. If the marketer's aim is to attract visitors, new businesses, and new residents, there must be a draw that the other cities can't claim.

The Grand Ole Opry, Country Music Hall of Fame, studios of cable television's popular Country Music Television Network, and the presence of so many successful stars help to underline the theme. In marketing terms, however, the city's attempt to look contemporary and appeal to presumed national preferences with an influx of national chain stores that have no connection to the city or to country music works against its interests.

To create marketing experiences, with all due respect to fine national hotel chains, it is smarter to call the main place of lodging the Opryland Hotel. Having noted that, the hotel cannot look like every other fine hotel except with a cowboy hat. It must reflect its special differences and engage the public by perhaps adding and integrating live country music performers (even if they are amateurs) such as singing clerks in the hotel shops and local retail stores and live music and dancing in a corner of establishments other than bars.

A city that calls itself Music City USA must deliver on its image by giving people music in more places than a CD player and the concert hall. A guitar-picker at the bus stop (who invites passersby to sing along) and a cappella groups well placed throughout the city's commercial section, performing the most requested songs, would enhance visitors' experiences and create more highly visible interactivity.

Along with putting performers' names on local businesses, playing their music, and projecting their song lyrics on walls or screens encourages visitors and shoppers to feel welcome and maybe even to sing along.

People stay longer and buy more when they feel part of what's going on and are invited to be more than spectators.

Nashville has more than a few museums (such as the Country Music Hall of Fame and Museum) that could benefit from more engagement with visitors, as opposed to strictly displaying impressive collections under glass. Staging related events allows visitors to share the mood and spirit of the Nashville life and the sound it sends around the world.

To live and work in a town where country music is the running theme, that point must be driven strongly as a way to keep and attract singers, musicians, songwriters, arrangers, publishers, music producers, recording engineers, talent managers and agents, musical instrument manufacturers and repair services, sound technicians, stage crews, costume makers, club owners and managers, and others who would hold, maintain and build upon the traditions as well as perform the necessary roles and tasks related to any of the above businesses.

Nashville and other cities or sites, like any subject of a marketing effort, must emphasize its own brand of quality, value, desirable location, colorful reputation, and enticing image—all of which remain important considerations in making travel or purchase decisions.

Just as Hollywood Boulevard, Tin Pan Alley, Rodeo Drive, and Rockefeller Center might draw people from everywhere who want to shop for shoes or eat a hamburger that might taste pretty much like hamburgers anywhere else, the sights, smells, sounds, and smiles that become the "Music City experience"—that come just from being there—are factors in determining the acceptance and success of a particular location.

While many well-known hotel chains and national restaurants might offer a degree of familiarity that suggests security and comfort, they often tend to be interchangeable with one another in the public mind and with their counterparts in other cities. People do not travel cross-country to stay at a hotel, eat at a restaurant, or shop at a store that reminds them of every other place they have been.

Marketers must understand that consumers cannot take away a feeling that a store is just a store or an office just an office. The experience created each time at each place and with each contact determines a product or an organization's success or failure. Clearly, some do it much better than others.

When one thinks of marketing, the hot new product or trend that is receiving the most attention usually come to mind first. Despite the innovation technology has brought, a museum or library typically gets listed among conservative, slow-to-change institutions, and the assumption is the marketing plan for such institutions must be serious, dignified, even highbrow. That assumption, while sometimes right, is mostly wrong.

Many of today's museums and libraries are just as likely to present an exhibit on the history of toys, licorice, beer, or vintage clothing as on World War I or seventeenth century art.

Museums often receive grants from foundations or funding assistance from corporate sponsors. Through the years many museums tied to special themes, from food production to space exploration or unique collections, have shaken the dusty archive images of old and become primary facilities for contemporary education, information, popular culture and, in many instances, for purely entertainment or promotional purposes.

From the Gene Autry Western Heritage Museum in Los Angeles to the Museum of Natural History in New York to the Smithsonian Institution Air and Space Museum in Washington, DC, to institutes dedicated to sports, cars, wars, the sea, toys, and much more, the museum has become culturally valuable and commercially significant.

Marketing is today an extremely important factor in launching, funding, sustaining, and attracting people to museums.

In Tennessee, Nashville's Country Music Hall of Fame and Museum offers a number of special exhibits in addition to its permanent ones, such as its tribute to Country Music Association Hall of Fame member Eddy Arnold. The exhibit was open to the public for six months in 2003 and was called, "I'll Hold You in My Heart: The Eddy Arnold Collection," named for Mr. Arnold's 1947 hit record, *"I'll Hold You in My Heart (Till I Can Hold You in My Arms)."* While 1947 sees like a long, long time ago, the exhibit attracted and fascinated crowds of tourists and local fans.

Included in the exhibit were 5,000 recorded radio shows; 2,000 photographs; 2,000 cans of film from Mr. Arnold's syndicated television series; 32 file-cabinet drawers of press clippings; 1,000 pieces of sheet music; numerous industry awards, gold records, business documents, posters, personal correspondence, musical instruments, memorabilia, recordings, personal items, scripts, and handcrafted presents from fans. Two items the museum considers to be highlights of the collection are the singer's customized Gibson J-200 guitar and his 1967 Entertainer of the

Year Award, the first ever presented by the Country Music Association.

As museum exhibits go, this one offered a solid career retrospective, assembled to appeal to, impress, and delight true fans of Mr. Arnold and of country music. To some visitors it was and will continue to be a touching tribute and a moving experience, perhaps comparable to looking through the singer's own family photo albums, closets, and drawers for personal touches that relate to his long, successful career. Others will be disappointed at the "traditional" museum collection presentation that respectfully arranges the items behind a glass wall and limits the experience to only viewing them. The one sign of movement or activity is from the strolling uniformed security guard.

For hundreds of years that is what museums did: they displayed collections and exhibited items of importance and value while admirers, students, and the general public looked on, at least two steps removed from the subject, though able to claim to have seen it.

But in the twenty-first century, people have come to expect more and museums must now compete for members, visitors, funds, and attention with a wide range of cultural events, entertainment programs, and interactive and multi-media presentations, all trying to show and tell their stories without the traditional dark or somber atmosphere. It is no longer a time for museums to operate as if they were only competing for members and visitors with other museums, art galleries, and the occasional lecture series.

The once staid repositories of interviews, papers, artifacts, photographs, and information are opening up in ways their directors and curators of days gone by might never have imagined.

The John F. Kennedy Library and Museum—Not Just Places to Keep Old Books

Dr. Edwin Schlossberg, the founder of Edwin Schlossberg Incorporated, a multidisciplinary design firm that specializes in interactive design for public places, notes, "Museums and large public attractions provide ways to create conversations about moments in the past, present, and future, and about ideas in any discipline. They provide the experiential base through which members of a society, at various levels of sophistication, can become part of the conversations about what is important . . .

> *"Each of the mass communication tools will be linked in some way in the next decades to create new communication experiences. The only way we can effectively orchestrate this development is by becoming connected with different-scale communities around us."*[1]

The John F. Kennedy Library and Museum is one example of Dr. Schlossberg's vision. Visitors not only view valuable historic items and papers, and have access to archives of material not available elsewhere, but they make their way through a recreated White House hallway. Doors off the hallway lead to replicas of the 1960 Democratic National Convention floor, a typical street in an American town during the campaign of 1960, the President's office, the attorney general's office, and a prime spot in front of the capitol to stand as a film begins of President Kennedy taking the oath of office and delivering his inaugural address.

Miniature recreations—basically stage sets—allow visitors to feel as if they are present at the scene, a part of history, and not just viewers of a newsreel and showcases full of history.

The presidency of John F. Kennedy was unique in that the young leader seemed to be at once charismatic and larger than life, yet friendly and approachable. In that sense, a museum exhibit that allows members of the public to come in closer is welcomed.

The marketing experience applied to the JFK museum conveys a feeling of being the proverbial "fly on the wall," of being present at important moments, moving through history and being exposed to what would become the legacy of John F. Kennedy's presidency.

After walking through a variety of pivotal scenes,

Exhibit 6.1:
Recreation of the Main White House Corridor

At the John F. Kennedy Library and Museum, visitors walk through a recreation of the main White House corridor leading to exhibits on the Peace Corps, President Kennedy's press conferences, civil rights, the Cuban missile crisis, and the space program.

Reproduced with the permission of Tom McNaught, Deputy Director, John F. Kennedy Library Foundation.

visitors are then offered the opportunity to become library members, attend regular lectures, panels, and special live programs led by noted historians. Members also have access to more than 8,400,000 pages of President Kennedy's papers; manuscripts containing some 34,000,000 pages; 180,000 photographs, as well

Exhibit 6.2:
Mock-Up of the
1960 Democratic National Convention Floor

John F. Kennedy narrates a 20-minute introductory film as visitors enter the museum galleries and step onto a recreated mock 1960 Democratic National Convention floor, complete with political signs, posters, and confetti at the John F. Kennedy Library and Museum.

Reproduced with the permission of Tom McNaught, Deputy Director, John F. Kennedy Library Foundation.

as video and audiotapes; and 15,000 objects from the Kennedy years.

A museum shop, catalog, and web site offer mementos of the experience, virtual online tours, books, posters, and souvenirs as reminders of the experience. Membership cards in the JFK Library also may be used for free admission to other presidential libraries.

Information and education are being marketed, along with a carefully presented image of a place and time in history that can shape or change one's opinions or perspective about a presidency or an era. The institute and its host organization also provide an opportunity to promote, display, or market a nearly endless array of related items that help to reinforce the museum experience.

A trip to a museum is now on a level with attending major events, such as plays or concerts. The efforts of the Kennedy Library and Museum is reflective of changes in the process and attempts by others to transform the research, study, and tour into an experience that brings the public inside and creates a connection.

Other museums and institutions worthy of note for creating effective marketing experiences:

- The South Florida Museum includes the Bishop Planetarium and the Parker Manatee Aquarium, and offers recreations of scenes from prehistoric times to the space age.

- *Les egouts (Sewers)—une vision souterraine de Paris (an underground view of Paris),* provides a truly inside look at one of the world's most famous, historic, and romantic cities by extending a warm invitation to take a "visit

Exhibit 6.3:
Recreation of the Television Studio Used for the
1960 Presidential Debate.

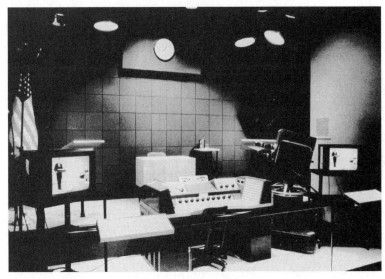

At the John F. Kennedy Library and Museum, visitors view an exhibit that replicates the television studio where the Kennedy-Nixon debates were produced.

Reproduced with the permission of Tom McNaught, Deputy Director, John F. Kennedy Library Foundation.

with specialist guides to the heart of the Paris waste water drainage network—A museum and an audio-visual show." The city that invites people to visit the Louvre, the Eiffel Tower, and the Cathedral at Notre Dame, also offers guided tours of the Paris sewer system. Educational and informational? Most

Exhibit 6.4:
Recreation of John F. Kennedy's Office

A recreation of the Oval Office during the Kennedy Administration.

Reproduced with the permission of Tom McNaught, Deputy Director, John F.
Kennedy Library Foundation.

definitely—and certainly sure to be an
experience.

- A trip to Chicago's Lincoln Park Zoo is no
longer a matter of standing behind a rail and
watching animals go about their business.
Programs such as the annual Zoo Lights Festival, which takes place each night from late
November through New Year's, offers chil-

dren and adults the experience of viewing dazzling displays of colorful lights, ice-sculptured holiday scenes, and brightly decorated homes. Other activities include puppet shows, ice carving, building gingerbread houses, holiday crafts, and train rides around the zoo. Costumed guides and musical entertainers help create a holiday experience and an atmosphere reminiscent of Toyland. Zoo memberships are available; non-member admission fees generate revenue and a full line of zoo-related merchandise is on sale. A popular Simon and Garfunkel song from an earlier day began with the words, "Something tells me it's all happening at the zoo . . . " and several zoos want to make it an experience.

Notes

1. Quotes attributed to Dr. Edwin Schlossberg are from *Interactive Excellence: Defining and Developing New Standards for the Twenty-first Century* by Edwin Schlossberg. New York: The Library of Contemporary Thought/ The Ballantine Publishing Group, 1998.

7

The Entertainment Marketing Experience

From the movies and TV to restaurants and back again
. . . sort of. Food that represents a film tie-in can be
fun and taste great at the same time. Meanwhile, in
an earthly place called Las Vegas, space aliens and
heroes gather to celebrate art, hobbies, curiosity,

fascination, and a consumer-driven marketing experience on a truly grand scale.

The Bubba Gump Shrimp Company Restaurant and Market

It all started with a movie. Life imitating art.

The 1994 motion picture *Forrest Gump* explained that, "Life is like a box of chocolates. You never know what you're going to get." Along with this wisdom the movie introduced a group of memorable fictional characters that included Mama, Jenny, and Lieutenant Dan. But after the title character, perhaps no one was more unforgettable than Bubba, Forrest's army buddy who he recalls, ". . . taught me about the shrimpin' business and how much I enjoy bein' around nice folks and all."

Fans of the film will remember the earnest, solemn presentation of the facts of life, according to Bubba, *"Shrimp is the fruit of the sea . . . you can barbecue it, broil it, bake it, sauté it. There is shrimp kabobs, shrimp creole, shrimp gumbo, pan fry, deep fry, stir fry. There's pineapple shrimp, lemon shrimp, coconut shrimp, pepper shrimp, shrimp soup, shrimp stew, shrimp salad, shrimp and potatoes, shrimp burgers, shrimp sandwich . . . That's about it!"*

Fans will also recall that after Bubba's untimely demise in the war, Forrest returns home and puts what he learned to work for him, honoring the memory of his friend by calling his business the Bubba Gump Shrimp Company. The company became a cash cow—or a cash shrimp, as the case may be—and a major device that advanced the story.

One thing executives of Hollywood studios know is how to take advantage of a moment, such as when a movie becomes so successful as to endear itself to the public. Few Hollywood studios know this as well as the Paramount Pictures unit of Viacom, which had mastered movie cross-sell-exploitation-merchandising years earlier with numerous films, particularly the *Star Trek* franchise of multiple television series, movies, books, and merchandise to fit any need, taste or occasion.

Bubba Gump Shrimp Company was unique, lending itself to not only the usual movie tie-in merchandise of shorts and caps, but to a lengthy list of potential things to do with shrimp.

Viacom Consumer Products, the licensing division of the entertainment conglomerate, approached Rusty Pelican Restaurants with a plan to design a restaurant that would combine quality seafood and a casual family atmosphere, developed around the theme of Forrest Gump's life, philosophy, and love of shrimp. The resulting concept was the first and only casual restaurant chain based on a motion picture property.

Like the film, Bubba Gump Shrimp Company

Exhibit 7.1:
Bubba Gump Shrimp Company Merchandise

Reproduced with the permission of Cathy Peterson, Bubba Gump Shrimp Co., Inc.

Restaurant & Market was an instant success. The restaurant also served as a marketing experience, providing an entertaining setting and good food, while continually reinforcing the film, video, DVD, books, soundtrack CDs, and related merchandise.

———

Exhibit 7.2:
Bubba Gump Shrimp Company–Miami

Reproduced with the permission of Cathy Peterson, Bubba Gump Shrimp Co., Inc.

The restaurant itself has a charming down-home décor that is reminiscent of the film's Alabama setting, with movie memorabilia and still photos lining the walls, as well as reproductions of script pages and scrawled "Gumpisms" covering the varnished table-tops. Guests of the restaurant can also try on plaster casts of Forrest's running shoes at a recreation of the movie's famous bus stop bench.

Shrimp is the number one fresh and frozen seafood in the United States, with Americans consuming about

Exhibit 7.3:
Actor posing as "Forrest Gump"
in the company's Chicago restaurant

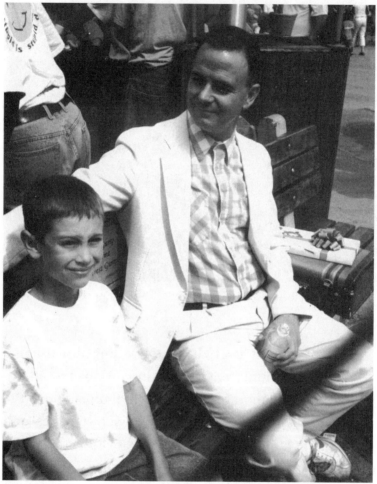

Forrest Jones (left) meets "Forrest Gump" as an actor steps into the role of the film character to welcome folks at The Bubba Gump Shrimp Company.

Reproduced with the permission of Cathy Peterson, Bubba Gump Shrimp Co., Inc. and Kristin Jones.

a billion pounds of shrimp each year. Bubba Gump Shrimp Company by 2004 had 14 restaurants in the United States, Japan, and the Philippines, selling approximately 800,000 pounds of shrimp per year. Plans called for growing the chain to as many as 50 restaurants by 2008.

The successful movie became a successful restaurant featuring menu items that include Mama Gump's Garlic Bread Basket, Lt. Dan's Drunken Prawns, Bubba's Far Out Dip, and assorted seafood delights. Ultimately, the entire venture proved to be a very successful marketing experience that should continue to promote the film, food, home video, and products tie-ins for years to come.

Clearly every company or organization does not have the resources of Paramount Studios or Viacom, but every company does not have to build or maintain an operation on such a scale. Examining how the cross-selling and partnering of companies and products can create and support a marketing experience works to the advantage of virtually everyone concerned.

Star Trek—A Prototype for Creating a Marketing Experience

A little boy in the 1950s might put on his Davy Crocket cap and imagine he was the King of the Wild

Frontier; a cape and a pair of tights transform a child into Superman; little girls become princesses, rock stars, doctors, or stars of the ballet . . . All it takes is a good imagination and the right outfit and props. When presented well, books, movies, and TV shows open doors to secret places to which children can escape to be different, fantastic, or simply someone else.

The entertainment industry creates the fantasies and through promotions, merchandising, and imagination children can experience the fantasy. Few creations have had the impact of Gene Roddenberry's *Star Trek,* the futuristic space adventure with the mission to boldly go where no man has gone before . . .

The original TV show was a surprise hit, developed a cult following, but ratings slipped, and the show was cancelled. Fans refused to accept that the vision of the future as presented was now just part of the past. They organized, rallied, and with a little help from members of the show's cast and crew, and with Mr. Roddenberry's blessing, the television show (and several sequels and spin-off series, as well as a succession of very successful movies) went on.

Star Trek's spaceship Enterprise crew did battle with enemies and aliens throughout the galaxy. The show was one of the first to build a cult-like following (called Trekkies) who learned the program's fictional languages and rituals, as well as adopted the clothing and makeup to emulate their favorite characters. Still,

Exhibit 7.4:
Star Trek Convention Web Site

Reproduced with the permission of Gary Berman, Creation Entertainment.

OFFICIAL STAR TREK LAS VEGAS CONVENTION

Star Trek Lives Large in Vegas!

Creation Entertainment proudly joins forces with our friends at Paramount Pictures, Star Trek: The Experience and The Las Vegas Hilton to present The 3rd Annual Official Star Trek Convention.

GUESTS:

APPEARING ON THE MAIN STAGE

WILLIAM SHATNER (Capt. Kirk)
LEONARD NIMOY (Mr. Spock)
COLM MEANEY (O'Brien of DS9 and ST:TNG)
NANA VISITOR (Major Kira)
DAVID GERROLD (popular writer of the classic Star Trek episode THE TROUBLE WITH TRIBBLES, David has also written many best-selling books)
LINDA PARK (Hoshi of Star Trek: Enterprise)
TOM HARDY (Shinzon of Star Trek: Nemesis)
ANTHONY MONTGOMERY (Travis Mayweather of Star Trek: Enterprise)
EUGENE RODDENBERRY (The son of Gene, and a creative force in his own right)
GARFIELD AND JUDITH REEVES-STEVENS (Authors DS9 "Millenium" series)
MARGARET CLARK (Executive Editor Pocket Books)
MARCO PALMIERI (Editor Pocket Books)
PAULA BLOCK (Executive Director of Licensing for Publishing, Viacom Consumer Products)
TERRY ERDMANN (Author "DS9 Companion")

AUTOGRAPH ROOM GUESTS:
We're very happy to welcome celebrities to The Official Star Trek Convention. They will be on hand throughout the weekend, taking part in activities, and also present at their booths in the vendor's room meeting fans and signing autographs for a nominal fee.

CONVENTION EVENTS:

- **POCKET BOOKS PRESENTATION:** a special panel on Star Trek publishing is set for

Sunday and participating will be:

- WILLIAM SHATNER (Author "Captain's Blood" and "Captain's Peril" announcing his new book)
- GARFIELD AND JUDITH REEVES-STEVENS (Authors DS9 "Millenium" series)
- MARGARET CLARK (Executive Editor Pocket Books)
- MARCO PALMIERI (Editor Pocket Books)
- PAULA BLOCK (Executive Director of Licensing for Publishing, Viacom Consumer Products)
- TERRY ERDMANN (Author "DS9 Companion")

- **SPECIAL VIDEO EVENT:** One of the all-time Creation highlights was welcoming the legendary **RICARDO MONTALBAN** (Khan) to our Grand Slam Convention in Pasadena (on two different occasions). Ricardo was as gracious and entertaining as you'd hope a Hollywood icon would be! Now, Mr. Montalban has generously agreed to film an all-new video piece for us to show at the Las Vegas Official Star Trek Convention. He will reminisce about playing Khan, being part of the Star Trek Universe, and discuss the re-opening of The Ricardo Montalban Theatre in Los Angeles.

Paramount Star Trek Project/Art Coordinator PENNY JUDAY will be joining the festivities in Vegas with a special presentation on STAR TREK props, how they are made, the difference between dummies and heroes. She will also discuss location shooting, going from script to screen, how the art department works, production and set design, and much more! Go inside the worlds of Star Trek! Penny will do 2 segments, one Saturday, one Sunday as follows:

STAR TREK PUBLISHING: Literary Star Trek has made publishing history, and we'll have a unique panel discussion on this amazing success story.

startrek.com is the source for Star Trek news for fans around the globe and we're thrilled to say that the wonderful folks at startrek.com will be taking an active role at this year's convention. We're in the talking stages now about specific plans but after our recent brainstorming session we are so excited: we'll keep you posted in this space!

- **GIANT DEALERS ROOM:** Nowhere else can you get the outstanding array of STAR TREK and sci-fi media collectibles... Vendors are coming from all around the globe to be on hand for the world's largest Star Trek Convention. Come to browse, come to swap, come to buy!

WILLIAM SHATNER & LEONARD NIMOY TOGETHER IN A PHOTO FOR YOU: This is a truly incredible unprecedented never before offered opportunity! Bill and Leonard have agreed to appear in photo ops TOGETHER (which will be full color 8 by 10's with a great background) with YOU! Extremely limited, please order quickly: **$199**

WILLIAM SHATNER: $70	**ROBERT DUNCAN McNEILL: $40**
LEONARD NIMOY: $70	**ALICE KRIGE: $40**
TIM RUSS: $40	**LINDA PARK: $40**
ETHAN PHILLIPS: $40	**TOM HARDY: $30**
NANA VISITOR: $40	**ANTHONY MONTGOMERY: $40**
WALTER KOENIG: $40	**WIL WHEATON: $40**
KATE MULGREW: $50	**CIRROC LOFTON: $40**
BRENT SPINER: $60	**JEFFREY COMBS: $30**
COLM MEANEY: $50	**CASEY BIGGS $30**
GEORGE TAKEI: $40	**VAUGHN ARMSTRONG $35**
MARINA SIRTIS: $40	**CHASE MASTERSON $35**
	MAX GRODENCHIK $30

CREATION TICKETS
217 S. Kenwood Street
Glendale, CA 91205

they needed somewhere to take them. Another planet seemed impractical. These people were adults with day jobs—real jobs—and families. Yet, they had pledged allegiance to *Star Trek* and to help create a better solar system for everyone.

Fans took their program very seriously and the *Star Trek* convention was born. People from around the world (most of whom had, of course, never met) organized conferences, exhibits, film retrospectives, seminars, readings, reenactments, and recruited former members of the TV cast to appear and lend authenticity to the experience.

They were promised an experience: an event with personal interaction, networking, films, books, fashions, memorabilia, celebrities, and non-celebrities—all brought together relating and connecting to a common theme.

Brand Preferences and Marketing Experiences: Lifestyles

From playthings to pin-up girls, brands must distinguish themselves to stand out in some very crowded categories. A child's doll evolved into an industry including dining, theater, and retail clothes. Another girl became an icon for a generation, proving beauty queens and beer are a winning, if unlikely, combination.

American Girl—These Dolls Are Much More Than Kids' Stuff

There are people who would claim there have been dolls for little girls perhaps as long as there have been little girls. Some have cried, some said "mama," some closed their eyes, and some wet. But it was not until the wizards of marketing and advertising saw the opportunities in a child being able to change a doll's clothes—from fresh diapers to designer gowns—that an opportunity became an industry.

Many people believe it started most significantly with Barbie. Named for its creator's own young daughter, the little toy doll changed the place of dolls in the toy industry and changed several other industries as well. Five-year-old girls began developing a sense of fashion and learned what being "stylish" was, asking questions about accessories and their role in dressing and maybe even in life. Barbie became a symbol of how many people in American society defined beauty, sex, and perhaps even their values.

A group of middle-aged women pointed proudly to their Barbie dolls. Once a small, childhood plaything, the curvaceous and multi-accomplished plastic Barbie has over several decades distinguished herself by achieving unimaginable success as, among other things, a fashion model, a college student, a rock star, a pilot, a doctor, a teacher, a bride, an aviatrix, a hair stylist, an Air Force officer, an Olympic medalist, an astronaut, a serious shopper, a ballerina, a dental hygienist, a goddess, the Princess of Ireland, and a Radio City Rockette—all before reaching the age of 40.

Now, a mature but still beautiful "small plastic woman figure of a certain age," Barbie is more than a fantasy plaything—she's a "collectible."

Marketers have for generations spoken with reverence of the toy that at once delighted little girls, fascinated their brothers, brought both smiles and raised eyebrows to many parents, incited feminists, and amassed a fortune in sales, finding unprecedented success through brand extensions and licensing deals. The primary focus was on continually updating Barbie's expansive wardrobe, fashions, and accessories. But also included were global and multiple projects, such as cartoons, books, web sites, telephones, records and CDs, music players, videos, breakfast cereal, luggage, appliances, greeting cards, valentines, stickers, candy, games, puzzles, computer programs, educational programs, makeup, and much more.

Barbie was fun to play with, fun to dress, fun to collect, and a little toy that became an industry in itself, leading the Mattel Corporation in a myriad of directions and businesses. But alas, between the ages of little girl at play and adult collector, Barbie would become to most little girls another of yesterday's childhood toys.

As important a phenomenon as the Barbie doll has been, it is still a toy and most children outgrow their toys—even their favorites. Additionally, there was the marketing issue that put the child and the toy together, but never created much of a bond between them. Barbie is the kind of doll little girls dress, play with, enjoy, but do not cuddle or take to sleep with them at night. Marketers brought out flashing lights and loud music, but never seemed to develop the kind of "Barbie experience" that promoted an emotional connection between child and toy.

Little girls might hope to grow up to *look* like Barbie or have a fabulous wardrobe like hers and exciting adventures, but few kids really expected to look up one day in real life and see Barbie's sports car, sailboat, motorcycle, helicopter, SUV, camper, horse, and van parked in their driveways . . . next to the swimming pool. Creating a world of fantasy was okay for Barbie, but a bit too much for even very young real little girls to imagine.

Yet, in toy departments around the world, there was a wide array of dolls and numerous generic, less expensive Barbie knock-offs, but there was never a real alternative to Barbie, particularly as little girls grew older. Little American girls found something lacking in the grandly indulged daydreams and lifestyle of Barbie.

In 1986, a pleasant woman named Pleasant Rowland looked closely at Barbie and the other choices available to little girls and decided it was time for a change. She had grown up to be an elementary school teacher, TV reporter, and textbook author, and had now started a business called The Pleasant Company.

In 2003, Ms. Rowland told the *Chicago Tribune,* "I and the generation of women I grew up with really were the first generation to break through, as a group, a lot of the gender barriers. We had broken stereotypical roles for ourselves. But the toys for our daughters were still stereotypical," adding, "I wanted to provide a thinking girl's doll."[1]

In 1986, the first three American Girl dolls were introduced: pioneer girl Kirsten, Victorian-age Samantha, and a World War II era child named Molly. The dolls represented three nine-year-old girls, each from periods in American history when life and times posed challenges. The fictional girls were strong on character, and each girl's story was told in vivid detail in a series of six books that described accurately what life was like in the United States during those particular periods in history.

"Those stories tell of rewards of perseverance, the fact that a lot of our expectations are not met," Ms. Rowland notes. "They talk about the courage to face one's shortcomings or mistakes, the importance of family and loyalty to friends. They help understand issues of jealousy and of being left out."[2]

Observing that girls enjoy the dolls and clothes, moms approve of the values, and both are intrigued by the setting—a world where girls matter—Ms. Rowland describes her approach as "chocolate cake with vitamins."[3]

The American Girl doll is 18-inches high and has evolved from the initial three into more than 30 incarnations. New characters have been added along with an "American Girl of Today" doll that a child can order with her choice of hair color and skin tone. The company that early on was described as the "anti-Barbie" has been a major success since it began. From catalog sales totaling $1.7 million in its first four months, American Girl's annual earnings in 2003 were estimated at $350 million.

And because American girls of any age or era enjoy being dressed in style, each doll has a wardrobe of both period clothing and accessories and contemporary outfits.

Expanding the company and the American Girl brand has taken the direction of creating additional products and elements that, separately and cumulatively, can be virtual prototypes of the marketing experience:

Exhibit 8.1:
American Girl Dolls

American Girls shown with their "American Girls"

Reproduced with the permission of Stephanie Spanos, Senior Public Relations Associate, American Girl.

- The American Girls Collection includes a virtual library of books, eight diverse characters from America's past in the form of 18-inch dolls with accessories, based on a typical nine-year-old girl who lived during notable times in America's past. Some 10 million American Girl dolls were sold through the company's catalog, retail stores, and web site between 1986 and 2004.

- More than 100 million American Girl books have been sold since the company's launch in 1986.

- A separate line of children's clothing and accessories are offered to match those provided for the dolls so that children and their dolls can dress alike.

- *American Girl* magazine is available on newsstands or by subscription with a special personalized souvenir issue included. Girls can read about kids like themselves who share their interests, and read advice and ideas on fun things to do and ways to get more from American Girl products. In 2004, the magazine had more than 650,000 subscribers, making it the eighth largest children's magazine in the U.S. and the largest

Exhibit 8.2:
American Girl Dolls

American Girl merchandise

Reproduced with the permission of Stephanie Spanos, Senior Public Relations Associate, American Girl.

publication dedicated exclusively to girls in the 7 to 12 age range.

- *American Girl* magazine receives more than 10,000 pieces of reader mail after the publication of each issue.

- Advice guides are published on subjects from setting a table, staying home alone, and hiding pimples to recovering from embarrassing incidents.

- The American Girl web site, *americangirl.com*, receives an average of 1.3 million visitors every month.

- American Girl Place, the company's first retail and entertainment site, opened in Chicago in 1998 and less than five years later was grossing an estimated $35 million annually—moving merchandise at twice the rate of the average retailer on Chicago's high-end "Magnificent Mile" shopping strip. By early 2004, the complex had welcomed more than 7 million visitors, guests, and shoppers, had served over 800,000 meals in its café, and entertained some 400,000 guests in its theater. The first American Girl Theater production was an original musical by Elizabeth Richter, an Emmy award-winning producer who also developed television pilots and music CDs for the company. A second location, American Girl Place New York, opened in 2003, welcomed more than 775,000 visitors and guests in its first six months.

- *American Girl Fashion Shows* are presented to offer nonprofit organizations a fundraising event that leverages the appeal of the American Girl brand to raise funds for children's charities. A combination entertainment and educational experience, American Girl events have generated millions of dollars for

Exhibit 8.3:
American Girl Musical

The cast of "Circle of Friends, An American Girl Musical"

Reproduced with the permission of Stephanie Spanos, Senior Public Relations Associate, American Girl.

good causes throughout the United States since 1992.

American Girl is an American success story. It's a company that produces, publishes, and markets quality products and has effectively developed its own lines of distribution—retail, catalog, and online—all aimed at creating an interaction and an emotional connection with consumers. It did not redefine the toy business or the retail clothing business, nor did it invent restaurants, theaters, books, or videos. But the company and its founder saw an opportunity, *created a niche,* and developed a market, bringing entertainment and education to young girls between early childhood and adolescence, a group that was not being well served by existing companies.

In 1998, Mattel, the world's leading toy maker (and the maker of Barbie) acquired American Girl. Many observers thought this a good business decision, finding a unique compatibility between the two brands as well as a complementing product lines. Each brand, however has been addressing its target markets separately. The marketing experiences and customer relationships created by American Girl, with the resources of its corporate parent, should only grow stronger over time.

How relevant is this example when compared to a "typical" new business start-up or a marketing case study?

It is reasonable to suggest that most new businesses begin with ambitious goals, some obviously more realistic than others. Whether entrepreneur or seasoned professional trying to repeat or expand on a successful resume, managers and marketers start with an idea, a dream, a plan, and the ability to provide or generate the resources necessary to get the venture underway.

While it is unlikely that an average company or organization might aim for as widely diversified a product line as American Girl's toys, clothes, books, restaurants, theaters, and more, remember that American Girl did not start out as a $350 million a year unit of a giant corporation. It began as a small Wisconsin-based company with an idea to make dolls for young girls.

Pleasant Rowland wanted to create a doll that would be viewed by the public as filling a void in the market, not like any other doll being sold. She also wanted her young consumers to feel a connection to the doll and wanted the doll to be a tool for helping a girl learn and feel good about herself.

An examination of the many directions in which it might or could evolve identified opportunities to create marketing experiences that would bring the products, company, and consumers together.

It is not the size and capitalization of the company or even the product that inherently determines success. In this instance, it was identifying that something was missing in the market and acting creatively on that discovery.

The company also understood what little girls wanted and what would make a difference to them. Finally, it was having the vision to conceive the product and pursue innovative ways to help it succeed. Vision, innovation, and determination contributed to the experience. The same process of having or discovering an idea, and moving forward to implement it should be a process applicable to other companies, organizations, and issues both large and small.

Miss Rheingold and Her Beer

To many people, brand preferences continue to be a mystery when it comes to certain products such as beer, coffee, cigarettes, bathroom tissue, or aspirin. Particularly to people who are not regular consumers of a product, the brands seem to be pretty much interchangeable—*beer is beer and it all tastes the same*—with the packaging and prices appearing to be the only points of differentiation. Even an independent testing laboratory study declaring one toothbrush the best among many makes no sense to these people. "It's a *toothbrush*—bristles attached to a plastic stick," they shout. "How different do these things need to be?"

That is why marketing, branding, advertising, and public relations exist—to bring these differences to the attention of consumers.

As with many products, demand must be created for both the public and the highly influential individuals and groups of retailers and distributors. Consumers cannot buy a bottle of a particular beer unless the distributor and the retailer choose to make that brand available to them. So what appears on the surface to be a rather standard advertising/marketing/promotional challenge is actually a very important business-to-business issue. Creating public demand is essential, but convincing the people who own or control already crowded shelves that there is room for one more is a separate and extremely critical issue, if not a wholly separate campaign.

On the dealer level, few inducements are as effective as money. That doesn't mean an envelope of cash is recommended, but distributors and retailers are business people with expenses and the producers who can lessen those expenses are usually the most welcome.

In the case of the largest industry brewers, tens of millions of dollars allocated for heavy media advertising campaigns, long-running promotions, and maintaining long-held relationships that carry a lot of weight. Independent, smaller microbreweries have essentially the same challenge as independent manufacturers of virtually any product in industries dominated by large, well-established brands.

To get the attention and support of distributors and retailers the independents must approach them with solutions to their problems: deep discounts, bonuses, advertising support, displays, promotions that will drive traffic, making consumers demand the brand so the retailers and distributors can simply respond to that demand and not undertake a major hard-sell push of the product, which might come at the expense of a product that may be easier to move.

A fairly standard promotion by breweries is to designate their brands regionally, such as declaring it "Chicago's beer" or "St. Louis's number 1 beer." Usually beer drinkers want more than that.

More than a half-century ago in New York, Rheingold Beer came up with a promotion that successfully engaged consumers, ending in 1963 when the brand disappeared. But with the dawning of the twenty-first century, both the beer and the promotion were positioned for a comeback. The beer had a new owner and the promotion was the now semi-legendary competition to become . . . *Miss Rheingold!*

The original event took place in the greater New York area, and in the 1950s helped make Rheingold Extra Dry Lager Beer one of the most popular brands in the market. The promotion was extremely popular locally and, because New York was the broadcast media center of the United States, whenever a television star such as Jackie Gleason, Milton Berle, or Jack Paar would refer to someone as a finalist for the "Miss Rheingold" title, America laughed—even when it didn't know why.

The late Malcolm Forbes, the colorful editor of *Forbes* magazine, reminisced as late as 1986, asking

Exhibit 8.4:
Miss Rheingold Print Ad, 1958

Madelyn Darrow, Miss Rheingold 1958

Reproduced with the permission of the Rheingold Brewing Company.

readers, "Do you remember the Miss Rheingold contest? When we came of beer-age five decades ago, the most talked about brew was Rheingold. For a whole year its ads featured a gamut of beautiful gals contesting for your vote to win election as that year's Miss Rheingold. It was fabulous advertising, and when it ceased, so did the popularity of the beer—although my recollection isn't clear as to which came first at the last. Wouldn't it be great if some national brand, beer or other, got us all involved in balloting for this year's most beautiful Miss?"[4]

Back then the contest drew millions of ballots. But Mr. Forbes might have been having a bit of sport with his readers as, the *Miss America, Miss Universe,* and *Miss USA* pageants notwithstanding, naming a woman "the year's most beautiful Miss" in 1986 would have been considered very politically incorrect. The Women's Movement gained momentum during the 1970s and '80s, and competitions won or lost based on looks were decidedly out of fashion and strongly under attack.

Nonetheless, as Mr. Forbes correctly noted, the campaign did provide a year of "fabulous advertising" and helped to sell a lot of beer.

On the web site *beerHistory.com*, a resident of East Harlem in New York City during the 1940s and 1950s recalled, " . . . running from store to store, grabbing as many ballots as I could. In the neighborhood there sure

Exhibit 8.5:
Miss Rheingold Print Ad, 1959

Reproduced with the permission of the Rheingold Brewing Company.

wasn't talk about the election for mayor or governor . . . but when it came to the Miss Rheingold Contest, everybody was involved. The talk was all about it. Everybody talked about it . . . and everybody voted."[5]

Large breweries made smaller, local beers such as Rheingold unprofitable, but in more recent years many microbreweries have been winning local support and attracting a variety of beer lovers looking for something more distinctive or exclusive by offering choices of flavors and brands.

The company's new owners strike a note that they believe will resonate with New Yorkers. Writing on the company's web site, Rheingold Brewing Company CEO Tom Bendheim acknowledges it's good to be back. "We've missed New York, missed the streets at night, missed the music, and missed seeing old friends and meeting new ones over a cold beer. It's been a long time and we're excited to be home.

"We're ready to have some fun, let loose, and we hope you'll join us . . . Rheingold is friends, music, the wee hours, and enjoying a good cold beer. Look for us when you want to make it a little more fun, a little louder, and a little later."[6]

Clearly setting the tone, such ads, letters, and web site messages allude to a brand marketing effort aimed at differentiating Rheingold from the more sophisticated, "champagne of bottled beers" type of positioning. A new marketing strategy and a very updated

Miss Rheingold campaign is aiming to revive the 120-year-old Rheingold as the beer of choice for New Yorkers who take being New Yorkers seriously.

But far from reflecting the "wholesomeness" and girl-next-door qualities of the 1950s Miss Rheingold campaign, the thirteen semi-finalists in the new competition are tough talking, bartending ladies. The new image for the esteemed old beer company features women in T-shirts and a suggestion of raw sensuality.

The new Miss Rheingold will appear at events and on billboards. Back then, the winner was a classic All-American beauty," noted the *New York Times*. "The new Miss Rheingold will be one of New York City's bartenders, the kind of woman who is more likely to sport a tattoo than high heels and a swimsuit."[7]

The appearances, events, and Miss Rheingold competition itself are aimed at creating a marketing experience, wrapped in the company CEO's promise to "have some fun, let loose, and we hope you'll join us."

Could Miss Rheingold be instead Miss Starbucks or Miss Krispy Kreme? Miss Microsoft or Miss Wal-Mart? Miss (your local community retailer here)? Of course. With a different focus and a different spin (and possibly a different tattoo), the idea of focusing attention on a brand by inviting the public to engage with it in the spirit of fun is as viable and adaptable today as it was in the 1950s. As online voting replaced the old

Exhibit 8.6:
Contemporary Miss Rheingold Print Ad

A "Miss Rheingold" for the twenty-first century. Members of the public can see all 13 contestants and vote for their favorite at the company's web site.

Reproduced with the permission of the Rheingold Brewing Company.

store coupon/paper ballots, it is reasonable to expect that once consumers arrive at the company's Internet site, there might be some mention of other offers, other events, special promotions, and perhaps even another word or two about the product.

Notes

1. Quotes attributed to Pleasant Rowland appeared in *The New York Times Magazine* article, "Girls and Dolls" by Leah Eskin, July 20, 2003.

2. Ibid.

3. Ibid.

4. The quotation attributed to Malcom Forbes from 1986 was reprinted in the column "Thoughts on the Business of Life," Forbes magazine, May 26, 2003.

5. The web site www.beerHistory.com provided information about Rheingold beer.

6. Quotations are from the Rheingold Brewing Company web site: www.rheingoldbeer.com.

7. Quote appeared in *The New York Times Magazine* article "A Thirst Quenching New York tradition Is Being Revived" by Margaret Chiffriller, March 5, 2003.

CHAPTER
9

Brand Preferences
Marketing Experiences: Food

In the U.S.A., coffee and doughnuts—together—are
an American institution. Separately, they can be fascinating examples of the marketing experience. Two national chains that both began at separate times, when
the economy did not favor new business start-ups.

Separately they not only redefined their respective categories; it might be said they *reinvented* them.

Starbucks

There are many success stories in marketing, but there are obviously some that stand apart from the rest. A good clue as to who or what are the industry's true breakout stars is when marketers themselves cite a particular example by using it as a benchmark or the standard for success—as in, "This might be the next McDonald's," or later, "This will be bigger than eBay," or "This one could be another Starbucks!"

Just as American Girl did not *invent* the toy doll, but created a new twist on building the *connection* between a child and the American Girl doll, Starbucks did not invent the cup of coffee—nor did it originate the coffee house or coffee bar or coffee shop. Starbucks did, however, *re-define* the position of coffee and coffee lovers in one of the best and most successful and dramatic examples of a marketing experience in decades.

Many marketers list Starbucks first on their lists of winners, using pretty much the same phrase: "It wasn't that they were selling *coffee* as much as they were promoting *the experience of going to Starbucks* for coffee and more." Coffee is the product; Starbucks is the experience.

Additionally, there was a moment when Starbucks figuratively hit the marketing ball out of the park—when its success was unmistakably clear by the "genericizing" of coffee and taking ownership of the beverage. This would occur when someone would ask a friend or co-worker, *"Are you going for a Starbucks?"* rather than *"Are you going to Starbucks?"*

Similar situations exist with Coke, Kleenex, and Xerox, but very few others. The brand names became synonymous with the product or, in the consumer's opinion, becomes the new way to refer to the product whether the item is in fact that particular brand or not.

What did Starbucks do that other restaurants or brands of coffee or cafes did not do that made it both a preferred brand and a status symbol? Some might suggest the company "sold the sizzle, not the steak," in the same manner in which promoters try to get people out to a nightclub or a concert without knowing who will be performing, but knowing they like the venue and atmosphere. When people buy season tickets to a theater series, they do so at times before the series schedule is fully determined.

Starbucks's own stated objective is to become established as "the most recognized and respected brand in the world." By any measure, that is a large (or in Starbucks terms "Venti") objective. Its strategy is to keep expanding its retail operations, grow its specialty sales, and *pursue opportunities to leverage its brand by introducing additional products and developing new channels of distribution.*

Its tactics involve integrating its product or items that relate to its products into consumers' lives in as many ways as possible, beginning with the first cup of morning coffee, the cup in which it is served, the pot in which it was brewed, and continuing on through the day with recipes, reading material, snacks, an Internet connection, and perhaps a CD or two to provide enough background music to complement the experience.

A single success and a single successful marketing experience can be extremely challenging. How large, rich, talented, and organized does one have to be initially to aspire with a straight face to be "the most recognized and respected brand in the world"?

The process began to take shape reportedly with a single visionary executive who saw the product as a vehicle to marketing the experience of selling and drinking coffee. A consumer going into any of thousands of Starbucks locations, choosing a unique coffee beverage and perhaps a distinctive bakery item to accompany it, knows what to expect.

The public's perception of what Starbucks is and has to offer is reality regarding product, service, quality, and ambiance. The company has created a presence by focusing on integrating itself into the culture without the traditional television blitz such an achievement normally requires.

Not a venue to offer a private label product manufactured by one of the industry's usual anonymous producers, Starbucks developed its own beverage lines starting with its coffees—especially strong or exotic brews, cappuccino, latte, espresso, as well as cocoa and specialty teas in a multitude of variations. The company sold its coffees initially to fine restaurants, and then began selling straight to the public through its own outlets and direct distribution systems, primarily catalogs, direct mail, and the Internet.

The locations, carefully positioned in upscale, high traffic areas, suggested the style of expensive pastry shops or specialty stores usually located in fine hotels. The Starbucks stores were not restaurants, bakeries, coffee shops, or coffee houses of the type popularized in the 1960s but were, to an extent, rather a combination of *all* these types of establishments in a new package.

The décor and ambiance of the shop conveyed an easy, welcoming, yet dignified atmosphere appropriate for corporate board members, busy executives, academicians, students, and "ladies who lunch." By setting prices and claiming quality standards at "premium" levels, Starbucks hoped to appeal to, and limit, itself to a clientele willing to pay perhaps *triple* the cost of a regular cup of restaurant coffee, and to have the public know that fact right out front. Such snob appeal worked well for cars, jewelry, wine and other items, so why couldn't it work for coffee?

A trip to Starbucks or the appearance of someone holding an easily identifiable white and green Starbucks "take-out" cup made a statement about one's status, taste, and ability to afford something regarded as a premium-level product. The public had historically accepted that luxury items and personal indulgences cost more. Starbucks wanted to be perceived as both a luxury and an indulgence.

It is reasonable to suggest no one anticipated the level of success that was to follow the opening of the first Starbucks in Seattle's Pike Place Market in 1971. Howard Schultz joined the company in 1982 as director of retail operations and marketing. He would ultimately prove to be the person who would guide Starbucks through its explosive period of growth and success, as well as influence America's (and later, much of the world's) attitudes about coffee.

Starbucks was doing well selling its coffee to fine restaurants. While on a trip to Italy, Howard Schultz noted the popularity of espresso bars in Milan and saw the potential for developing a similar coffee bar culture in Seattle. He convinced the founders of Starbucks to test the concept in Seattle at a new separate location.

In 1985, Schultz founded Il Giornale, offering

brewed coffee and espresso drinks made with Starbucks beans. Two years later, with backing from local investors, his new company acquired the assets of Starbucks. He opened additional locations in Chicago and Vancouver, and changed the name of the expanded organization to Starbucks Corporation. (The name, in perhaps a wink at the type of high-end, literate customer it hoped to attract, was that of the first mate of the Pequod, the whaling ship that was the scene of most of the excitement and action in Herman Melville's classic novel *Moby Dick*.)

The next year Starbucks introduced its first mail order catalog, which created a national presence and a personal link to the consumer, providing service to all 50 states in the U.S. The company also established a relationship with CARE, the international relief and development organization, and introduced the highly successful CARE coffee sampler. It was an intelligent product offering that helped raise greater awareness of Starbucks and position it as caring and socially responsible with its target audience.

Starbucks became a publicly held company in 1992 with its stock listed on the NASDAQ trading system. That same year, the company began a major expansion effort that included opening coffee bars in Nordstrom department stores and in Barnes & Noble bookstores. With new outlets thriving in San Francisco, San Diego, and Orange County, California, as well as in Denver, Colorado, the number of Starbucks locations had grown to 165.

The decade that followed brought an explosion of steady and rapid growth for Starbucks throughout the U.S. and internationally, helped by the launching of the web site, *starbucks.com*, which brought special blends and gift baskets of products into homes around the world. It also helped to position the brand as the personal choice of millions of people worldwide who demanded something perceived to be a cut above most other coffee products.

Starbucks knew its market well. It defined its target audience and offered the complete experience: a comfortable place to get away for a brief time—usually accented with the sounds of soft jazz—where a variety of specialty coffee beverages and bakery products, biscotti, and European-inspired snack foods and high-end products were offered to enjoy there or to take home to prolong the experience. Quality coffee makers, servers, designer cups, mugs, and specialty pieces created for home use extended the Starbucks experience. Many were made for and sold exclusively through Starbucks.

Other stores offered quality merchandise, but Starbucks's focus was not only on making a sale, but on forming new and continuing customer and business relationships, ventures, partnerships, and agreements to enhance its status and image as the choice of people-in-the-know. All the while, its market base continued to expand.

More than three decades after its first appearance in Seattle, Starbucks continues to be a tasteful place for people to meet, enjoy a variety of coffee beverages and other specialty drinks, and feel very much in the company of other people who appear to appreciate the good things in life. The average Starbucks (even those tucked in corners of supermarkets) projects an almost salon-like atmosphere of good taste and civility that customers feel immediately.

The company recognized decades ago that some members of the public want more, will pay more, and enjoy an atmosphere that allows them to feel somewhat a part of a privileged class . . . for under five dollars.

The perception of Starbucks is that of a company that develops, produces, and sells quality products, and offers an atmosphere and experience many consumers enjoy and a product they know is not for everyone.

Starbucks premium coffees, once available only through the company's own stores and direct distribution outlets, have become more accessible in a variety of special blends through arrangements with leading companies and organizations that include:

- United Airlines
- Canadian Airlines

- Hyatt Hotels

- Westin (now Starwood) Hotels

- Chapters Inc. (the Canadian bookstore)

- Kraft Foods (extending the Starbucks brand into grocery channels across the U.S.)

- Albertson's (which added more than 100 Starbucks locations in its supermarkets since the year 2000)

- SAZABY (opening Starbucks coffee houses as part of a joint venture in Japan)

- And numerous others

By mid-2004 Starbucks was the world's leading specialty coffee retailer, operating and licensing more than 7,500 coffee shops in some 30 countries.

The company knows its market well because it had a major role in shaping and defining that market, most visibly targeting the emerging young upwardly mobile professionals (who were called YUPPIES in the 1970s and '80s when Starbucks was starting out).

Starbucks positioned itself to appeal to this target group and if it couldn't get enough of them, the company promoted the target group as a desirable segment of which to become a part. All it took to fit in was to become a Starbucks customer.

With little media advertising, Starbucks used pub-

Exhibit 9.1:
Coffeehouse Activities

Students stop by a coffee shop for a coffee drink and a wireless connection. Photograph: Karin Gottschalk Marconi.

Reproduced with the permission of Karin Gottschalk Marconi and Mary Kay Petrella.

lic relations, introductory coupons, word-of-mouth promotions, bulletin boards, in-store displays, and the high visibility of its carefully selected locations and signage to maximum advantage. Many Starbucks locations offered:

- Live music featuring local musicians (who could usually be counted on to invite friends who would then become more familiar with the local Starbucks and become regular customers).
- Coffee tastings featuring sample coffees from around the world with experts on hand to explain what makes a great coffee.
- Community events from exhibits to speakers to charity fundraising.
- Local initiatives and programs aimed at benefiting local communities and institutions.

Its message was it understood young professionals in a hurry, and with much on their minds, wanted particular products in a certain type of environment and atmosphere. Starbucks offered a place that *looked* like its customers wanted to look: successful, dignified, distinctive, and very cool.

And because it knows what its customers want and enjoy, Starbucks also:

- Acquired Hear Music, a San Francisco-based music company and in 1995, noting the popularity of its in-house music program, began selling its own music compilations on CDs.
- Began serving Frappuccino blended bever-

ages, a new line of low-fat, creamy, iced coffee drinks.

- Introduced "iced shaken refreshments," a handcrafted and refreshing new beverage category featuring coffee and tea shaken over ice.

- In 1996, in partnership with Dreyer's Grand Ice Cream, introduced Starbucks Ice Cream and Starbucks Ice Cream bars, which quickly became the number one brand of coffee ice cream in the United States.

- That same year, in a North American Coffee Partnership venture with the Pepsi-Cola Company, began selling a bottled version of Starbucks Frappuccino blended beverages.

- Installed and expanded high-speed wireless service, T-Mobile HotSpot, to more than 2,700 Starbucks stores.

- Began offering the Starbucks Card, a prepaid stored-value debit card for customers to use and reload.

- Launched the Starbucks Card Duetto Visa, the first-of-its-kind payment card blending Visa credit card functionality with the re-loadable Starbucks Card.

- Entered into an agreement with Host Marriott International to open coffee bars in select properties.

Starbucks seems to be everywhere—on corners, on campuses, in better hotels, in airports, on airplanes, in office complexes and shopping centers, as well as in department stores and neighborhood supermarkets—offering its target market segment distinctive non-alcoholic beverages that seem intended both to be enjoyed and to make a statement about the people who enjoy them.

To emphasize its sense of social responsibility, as well as promote greater interaction with and support for concerns shared by its customers, Starbucks:

- Formed an alliance with eight companies to make possible a gift of more than 320,000 new books for children through the All Books for Children annual book drive.
- Formed the "Out of the Park, Into the Books" partnership with baseball star Mark McGwire.
- Formed Urban Coffee Opportunities with "Magic" Johnson's Johnson Development Corporation, to develop Starbucks Coffee locations in underserved, urban neighborhoods across the U.S.

- With international business partners seeded the Starbucks Cares Fund with $1.2 million to benefit the September 11th Fund (customers and partners have contributed more than $1.4 million).

- Announced a $1 million partnership with Jumpstart, a national organization that pairs college student tutors with Head Start children.

- Created a partnership with Conservation International to promote environmentally sound methods of growing coffee and helped establish conservation efforts at several sites.

- Entered into an agreement with TransFair USA to market and sell Fair Trade Certified coffee, committing to the purchase of one million pounds of Fair Trade Certified coffee.

- Provided $1 million in financial support to coffee farmers through community investments.

- Celebrated Earth Day with a $50,000 contribution to the Earth Day Network.

- Through the Starbucks Foundation, awarded more than 650 grants totaling $6.5 million to literacy, schools, and community-based organizations across North America since 1997.

- Entered into a $225,000 commitment to America SCORES, a national nonprofit, youth development organization that uses the sport of soccer and literacy to inspire team-work among at-risk children in urban public schools.

- Offers the Doonesbury@Starbucks line of products with all net proceeds donated to local literacy organizations.

- Encourages more than 50,000 hours of part-ner and customer volunteer time and con-tributes $500,000 to nonprofit organizations across the United States and Canada through "Make Your Mark" volunteer program.

Clearly Starbucks is an unusual case in that its success was so enormous. But the fact that it began with a sin-gle product and a single location and grew to more than 7,500 outlets in 30 countries in less than three decades, indicates what can be done with a good idea, a vision of what is possible, a good plan, good man-agement, good marketing, and disciplined follow-through.

Management with vision and talent was alert to what others were doing, saw the potential of taking a simple idea from Europe and, after studying the market, adapted it, believed in it, and brought it to heights unimagined—perhaps by anyone except Howard Schultz.

Through the entire process Starbucks kept its eye on the customer, beginning with unique blends of coffee and the right atmosphere (a success); adding light foods and dessert items that went well with coffee (a success); adding music and selling CDs of the music customers liked best (a success); publishing a magazine (*not* a success); acquiring Internet access (a success); and offering secondary products that related to its primary product (such as coffee makers, coffee grinders, cups, serving pieces—all successes). These were products that allowed the consumer to engage with the company on a continuing basis—to make it part of their lives and routine.

It is important when hoping to become "the next Starbucks" to remember that the company did not have its growth surge overnight. Few overnight successes actually do occur overnight.

Everything is relative. If a marketer has a product that can benefit from adapting the Starbucks model, study it carefully. Adapt it. Rework it. As *going for a cup of coffee* became for millions of people *going for a Starbucks*, dreams are still worth dreaming.

Krispy Kreme Doughnuts—
An Old-Fashioned Product
Stays Fresh

The spelling of the product name is the type of pure advertising-ese that drives English teachers crazy. Children who have seen the boxes at home often enough and know what's inside are very likely to start school believing "crispy cream" is spelled *Krispy Kreme*. Fortunately for the company, success is not based on spelling skills.

The product has done well on its own since 1933 when a farmer and storeowner named Ishmael Armstrong bought the company and hired his nephew Vernon Rudolph as a door-to-door doughnut salesman. Vernon helped grow the family business into several successful stores with a customer base that could not get enough of the product. Krispy Kreme became a regional favorite in several U.S. southern states. And word continued to get around.

Television personality Rosie O'Donnell became such a champion of Krispy Kreme doughnuts that she would often have the sugary confections brought out on her daily national television show to be frosted, sugared, glazed, and sprinkled before drooling audience members. Without the usual lucrative endorsement deals, but for the sheer love of the product, some of the most celebrated figures have professed their love for Krispy Kreme doughnuts, including former U.S. president Bill Clinton, Oscar-winning actress Nicole Kidman, and basketball legend Michael Jordan.

A French chef in New Orleans developed the recipe. With eager customers watching the doughnuts coming fresh off an assembly line, they are quickly packed and sold while they are still warm. A neon light is illuminated as each fresh batch is produced and announces "Hot Doughnuts Now."

Earlier discussions of creating the marketing experience noted that many companies and businesses found they were able to attract attention and gain good will by positioning their creative talent up-front, usually in street-level store window. Pizza chefs, candy makers, hairstylists, portrait artists, and others would appear to be putting on a show as they worked in full view of the public. Few businesses took this approach as seriously as Krispy Kreme doughnuts.

Newsweek writer Catherine Skipp explained, "Krispy Kreme calls it 'doughnut theater.' And the sight and smell of one of its center-stage doughnut machines, which can fry and glaze as many as 2,600 doughnuts an hour, create such an opening day stampede that police are routinely needed to handle traffic snarls."[1]

The Winston-Salem, North Carolina-based company offers this "show-and-smell" aspect of its marketing presentation good naturedly, but behind the sizzle is a serious, well-crafted plan.

Marketing consultants Ben McConnell and Jackie Huba, founders of Wabash & Lake, believe the arrival of a new Krispy Kreme store is an *event*. They note, "Years spent cultivating customer goodwill, exploiting buzz opportunities, building friendly down-home relationships with the media, a go-slow growth plan, and a focus on bygone eras have paid off for Krispy Kreme. It has developed tidal waves of customer evangelism for a product with 11 grams of fat and 200 calories."[2]

Early in 2004, Krispy Kreme doughnuts was operating a hugely popular chain of doughnut shops with some 400 locations in 44 states and Canada. Much of the public remains unaware that the company offers more than 20 varieties of doughnuts, as its original glazed doughnuts have a virtual "cult status" among baked-goods fans and outsell by far all the company's other varieties combined.

But by mid-2004 many securities analysts were categorizing the company's stock as being in freefall.

In its first two years as a publicly held company, Krispy Kreme's stock price rose approximately 300 percent.[3] New store openings often attracted vast crowds of people who lined up to be among the first through the door to get the tasty treats early and still hot from the oven. Its menu is far more limited than some of its giant rivals, such as Dunkin' Donuts and

Starbucks, but Krispy Kreme does serve premium coffee and espresso drinks—and sells shirts, caps, and assorted merchandise bearing the company's logo to a fiercely loyal clientele.

Consider that many bakeries, popcorn vendors, and other purveyors of highly aromatic products have long had an advantage in attracting and seducing casual customers with their sensory appeal. But creating a marketing experience is more than just attracting public support by putting something that smells great in front of a fan and an open door. In the judgment of consultants McDonnell and Huba, Krispy Kreme has been able to win the hearts as well as the taste buds because:

- It starts with a hot product.
- It's not just fried dough; it's an experience, a "show" to enjoy.
- Customer communications drive product development.
- The company's roots are in grassroots marketing.
- It gives away doughnuts so that people will buy them.

Behind each of these points is a solid, direct program for listening to the market and responding with products, service, and an attitude that is responsive. On the downside is the fact that most companies and organizations are eager for a quick response and grass-roots marketing can be a painstakingly slow process. Certainly a comment on a TV program that makes the public aware that former U.S. President Bill Clinton, Michael Jordan, or Nicole Kidman swear by the product and each would go out of their way to have it, can have a huge impact on consumers (depending on their opinions of the prominent people doing the swearing). Publicity is a key generator of awareness and differentiates the subject from competitors.

The marketing experience—making that connection with the public—has a lot to do with being seen and heard and, particularly in the case of doughnuts, appealing to a sense of smell and taste. The product must be first-rate or word-of-mouth advertising won't get people to take the taste test.

By most measures Krispy Kreme doughnuts are regarded as "amazingly good." When people heard about them from major celebrities and then endorsed by friends who confirmed their great taste, the ability to see the doughnuts being made up close and hand-delivered fresh made a strong case. To be offered a free bite-size chunk of unusual varieties (such as cheese cake or pumpkin-flavored doughnuts), to taste them before buying, and to receive a hot fresh doughnut as a gesture of gratitude for waiting in line, more often than not reinforces the concepts of quality, service, and courtesy. The consumer concludes these are nice people to be around and orders a few dozen doughnuts. The consumer has experienced the quality, service, and courtesy.

So why the drop in the Krispy Kreme stock price?

Company executives blame the explosive success of at least two diet programs that received phenomenal attention and labeled doughnuts as the enemy of the weight-conscious.

There was also the sinking economy that encouraged consumers to cut back on indulgences.

Would the new low-carb Krispy Kreme doughnut bring back the nervous weight-watchers? Would an economic upturn stimulate the public's desire for tasty treats?

Maybe. But most highly publicized diet and exercise programs tend to be passing fads. People who love doughnuts and would walk a mile for a Krispy Kreme are not likely to be swayed by the high calorie count for long—they came for the taste, quality, and service. Besides, a thin, glamorous actress and one of the best-conditioned athletes in the world are not images that convey convincing evidence of the product's negatives aspects.

Marketers must read the plan: the objectives, strategy, and tactics. Most any obstacle can be overcome, but it must first be identified and acknowledged.

Reactive moves such as creating a low-carb doughnut for dieters will not likely be more successful, relatively, than offering smokers a lower tar and low nicotine cigarette. Some will try it, but most people make purchase decisions for specific reasons. To focus on creating a low-carb alternative to chase a trend, does not offer a message about quality and value. The positive effects, if any, are ignored in favor of debating issue points that might not be part of the plan.

Almost two-thirds of the Krispy Kreme locations are stand-alone units with drive-through service and are franchises. In addition, due to immense popularity of the product, the company also sells its doughnuts to retail grocery outlets and convenience stores.

As corny as it will sound to some people—and certainly unsophisticated among marketers favoring a highly innovative approach to marketing—one of the strongest points Krispy Kreme has going for it is that the public perceives it as a "nice" company staffed with nice people. For a time, a large food service company owned Krispy Kreme, cut corners, tampered with product quality standards and sales dived.

The current ownership and management let it be known that Krispy Kreme was returning to its old ways—putting its emphasis on quality and service— and sales spiked back up. This indicator of a customer base that responds well to terms such as "getting back to our old values" and "returning to the old-fashioned way" describes a constituency that perceives quality, service, courtesy, simplicity, and friendliness as important determinants when making purchase choices. It may be one of the more low-tech approaches to engaging, connecting, and creating a positive experience for the public, but a sound marketing strategy has always been to *give the customers what they want.*

Free samples are great for goodwill as well as for exposing more sides of the product. Having a product that is uniquely good enough for celebrities to endorse without compensation is a great bonus. Very often the reasons people choose certain brands as their "favorites," whether the category is doughnuts, cigarettes, beer, popcorn, or clothing, are reasons that can't be easily articulated. An emotional connection—something about that brand or company—connects on a level that will encourage people to pay more or travel farther for a particular something. Research will help identify those qualities, preferences, and motivating factors.

Stay focused. If there are value points to be made for the subject, make them. Don't apologize for having a good product and try to change it.

Notes

1. Quotation from "Hot Bytes, by the Dozen" by Catherine Skipp, *Newsweek* April 28, 2003.

2. Quotes attributed to Ben McConnell and Jackie Huba are from their book *Creating Customer Evangelists* by Ben McConnell and Jackie Huba. Chicago: Dearborn Trade Publishing, 2003.

3. Statistic references are from Hoovers Online Report: "Krispy Kreme Doughnuts," June 20 2004. www.hoovers.com.

CHAPTER 10

The Technology Marketing Experience

A book about creating the marketing experience should include information on companies that use the latest available technology for just that purpose. The tricky part is that technology is the one area, perhaps more than any other, where changes occur at such high speed that "the latest new thing" is likely to seem dated by the time the book is published (or soon after). By its very nature, technology is constantly changing, evolving, and updating its product to include or reflect a new discovery or a new version of an old favorite.

But as the technology rocket continues to gain speed, it is a relatively safe bet that the people who run a company called AEI Digital will be along for the ride, if not steering the ship.

AEI Digital

AEI Digital describes itself as an organization that creates prototypes—a creative agency providing media consulting and three-dimensional multimedia content to communicate its clients' vision and articulate their mission. It also says it is an agency composed of digital contractors, artists, technologists, and moviemakers.

What is *doesn't* say is that it offers what just might be the most effective and innovative application of technology to marketing to date.

This is "virtual reality" and it is essentially delivering what the futurists had been predicting was here for more than a decade, without being able to cite any specific examples, with the possible exception of IMAX movies.

AEI Digital is a subsidiary of the architectural firm

of EwingCole. The agency and the parent company work collaboratively to communicate and present their innovative representations of their clients' visions through architecture and multimedia solutions. AEI doesn't create the product; it creates an engaging *presentation* of the product—which sounds a lot like "marketing," though that is not one of the words the firm uses to describe what it does.

Securing investors, buyers, or tenants for a particularly unique building or development has always been a challenge. It can even be a challenge if the property is *not* unique, but conforms to the most familiar, successful, or utilitarian versions of what has been long accepted. Brochures with artists' sketches, usually enlarged to the size of theater posters, are mandatory props, as is a depiction of people enjoying and thriving in the scene, and a traditional plastic model that is supposed to show what the future building or development will look like when it is completed.

The fact is the brochures, posters, illustrations, videos, and plastic models (that often remind people of model railroad villages from their childhood), are largely there because *something* is needed for visual reference. It is the responsibility of the developers, architects, sales reps, and project visionaries to create excitement and enthusiasm for what is planned—for what could be. Sales tools and collaterals rarely accomplish that task alone or in combination.

The investor, buyer, or tenant is encouraged to "imagine" a shopping center, a hospital, a college campus, a resort, or a stadium with all the features, colors, and uniqueness a plastic model can convey. The more ambitious the project, the more elaborate the model . . . and the more there is to imagine. Digital technology offered the possibility of looking beyond the plastic miniature, of seeing what does not yet exist, as well as hearing the sounds, viewing a "virtual reality" in place of the various imagined versions.

The *New York Times* noted, "From ballparks to hospitals, digital models offer an advance walkthrough."[1] Using concepts evolved from movies and video games, the digital models create more than a picture: they show how a project might perform under various conditions.

Based in Philadelphia, Pennsylvania, and Irvine, California, AEI Digital was not the first company to use computers to attempt to bring model developments to life, but its work has been among the most dramatic. One such example is the $458 million ballpark of the Philadelphia Phillies. AEI Digital worked with EwingCole and the Phillies to create a detailed digital prototype of what would later be named Citizens Bank Park.

"Thousands of people toured the park," the *New York Times* reported, "in a sense, long before it existed. They visited it virtually, gliding through a finely detailed three-dimensional model . . . meticulously constructed in more than four million polygons . . . "[2] This gave the Phillies and their fans a virtual tour of the ballpark before it was built. Its digital imagery provided the basis for various ways of experiencing the park, using animations and still photographs, artists' renderings, and room–size mock-ups of luxury suites complete with field vistas and an interactive seating diagram. It was a cornerstone of the organization's marketing and sales efforts, and helped to sell out virtually all of the park's costly luxury suites at prices ranging from $115,000 to $200,000.

Imagine touring a ballpark with crowds of people in the seats, people in motion, vendors, the team members in their places—and not having to *imagine* it. Imagine such applications for projects and properties other than ballparks—imagine the virtual museum tour or the space center or the zoo . . .

It is technology applied to the marketing experience of the future in the most dramatic and effective way. And unlike much of what technology promises, it exists today.

Notes

1. Quotations from the New York Times first appeared in the article, "Touring the Future, Virtually" by Michael Marriott, March 4, 2004.
2. Ibid.

Postscript

A Crash Course in Creating the Marketing Experience

With all its different disciplines and approaches to a subject, marketing programs can have an almost infinite variety and much of what is said or written will be interpreted differently. This book is intended as a preparatory tool and a guide to creating a marketing experience. Certainly the possibilities don't end there. But for the busy executive in a hurry (or for the slow readers, also in a hurry), the next several pages present a general summary of the process as detailed up to this point. Take a quick look at it, then go back and read the book as time permits. Or, read the book and consider this an at-a-glance refresher without the examples or elaboration.

A point that keeps coming up is how people both in and out of marketing define and relate to the term differently, often using marketing interchangeably with the words packaging, advertising, public relations, graphic arts, event management, or sales. Of course marketing can encompass all that and more in a variety of combinations. Every marketing plan, even if all followed the same format, can be customized and written to include just the specific activities or disciplines that will address and achieve the plan's objectives.

Similarly, what constitutes a "marketing experience" will continue to be the subject of debate. Is an experience only interactive? Does it require physical participation between a consumer and the subject? Can laughing, crying, cheering, or some other verbal response be considered an experience? Test-driving a car is an experience, but can a daydream or fantasy in which someone imagines the thrill, pleasure, comfort, pride, or exhilaration of driving a car be an experience?

A person throwing or hitting a ball that travels a long distance and finally stops with a great impact has power. Words have power. Imagination has power. Illusion has power. Is it necessary that power always be of equal proportion or degrees before it can be said to exist?

Someone loses twenty pounds over three months with strenuous exercise, while someone else loses the same weight over the same amount of time by significantly reducing their intake of foods high in calories and fats. Did one person have an experience and the other not?

Marketing, like so much else, can get bogged down or derailed when experts focus on the terms and nuance more than on the action and the results.

Consider the amusement park ride that propels a person to great heights, turns sharply, then plummets at breathtakingly high speed, and repeats the process several times in a short period. Exiting the ride, the person pauses for a moment to regain a sense of balance and equilibrium.

Now imagine a person at a theme park climbing aboard one of the virtual thrill rides, such as the "Star Tours" ride at Disney World or the "Back to the Future" ride at Universal Studios. Both rides use combinations of sensory imagery—film, sound, mirror-effects, and a motorized chair—to create the illusion or sensation of propelling a person to great heights, turning sharply, then plummeting at what seems to be breathtakingly high speed, and repeats the process several times in a short period—all while the person and the "ride" remain in place. Which person walks away feeling as if he or she just had an exciting, heart-racing experience?

Of course the answer is *they both did.* One was real, while the other created the illusion of being real, but basically, "they did it with mirrors."

A marketing experience can be intensely physical or strongly emotional, but the one that qualifies as the *true* marketing experience is the one that works. The objective is to achieve the objective, not to argue about the literal definitions of the processes.

This book has presented information and examples of marketing experiences. For marketers on the go, this "cheat sheet" explains the Marketing Experience in brief.

- The most effective marketing programs engage the consumer and create a connection or a presence, often without people even realizing that is what's happening.

- A brand, product, issue, or subject can enter consumers' lives and consciousness, to a point where the brand's logo or label is no longer noticed, but the consumer is very much aware it is there.

- Creating a marketing experience is the process of developing a connection that links the product, the brand, the company, a person, or an issue that is the subject of a marketing effort.

- Marketers need to understand the uniqueness of each market segment and why what motivates some people has no effect on others.

- It is important to know the market and understand the various methods and processes that will appeal to distinct market segments, such as people with specific lifestyles, as well as ethnic, religious, and socially-conscious groups.

- Market segments are distinguished by a variety of factors including age, income, gender, geographic or regional ties, hopes, and fears. This has been widely known for decades, yet some marketers continue to employ a "mass" market mentality, as if one size fits all. It doesn't.

- Experienced marketers understand that companies and clients, as well as segments of the public, believe whatever they are presenting to the market should be the newest version of what they can offer or something that favorably compares to the newest version. The opposite of new is old, a term which marketers have difficulty treating in a positive context.

- Companies need to keep the members of their various constituent groups engaged, loyal, and coming back, but need new people both to sustain their organizations and to help them grow.

- Advertising—particularly television advertising—is extremely effective, though costly. Much of the public has a high degree of skepticism about what they see on TV, yet it is accepted that advertisers deal in fantasy and people still want to believe that dreams can come true.

- Marketers also use fantasies in presentations as a device to learn more about the consumer mind and desires. Knowing what people are willing to believe is an important step in selling products or in winning support.

- While "truth in advertising" must be taken seriously, creative advertising also gives consumers "permission to believe" virtually anything is possible. The public does not believe that cars fly or that dogs can talk, but those are not the types of ads that generate complaints.

- Pop psychology programs have for years promised consumers that using the power of both the conscious and subconscious mind will help them to realize their goals. *Visualization is the first step toward making desire become reality.* The degree to which people are willing to suspend belief is significant in creating a marketing experience.

- The marketing experience can be an event, an ad, or an acknowledgment that enables people to relate willingly to the message and connect with its appeal, experiencing a sense of excitement, pleasure, or satisfaction.

- Creating an experience and a connection with consumers should be a goal of most marketing efforts. Some type of interaction that invites the public to be a participant rather than a spectator promotes a bond with consumers.

- The term *experiential marketing* refers to marketing efforts that engage consumers or other segments of the public, causing them to feel an emotional and psychological as well as a physical connection to the subject.

- Seasoned marketers disagree about whether or not all experiences relating to the sales process or brand development qualify as *experiential marketing.* One side says a direct interaction is required, while others believe an emotional response should also be considered an experience—hence experiential.

• The more successful marketers take action, rather than spending the budget and productive time debating theories. Research should determine the direction of a marketing program based on the public's attitudes and preferences, not those of the marketers.

• Like so many other aspects of marketing, a marketing experience can in fact occur on many levels. It can be psychological, tapping into emotional or sensory feelings, nostalgia, daydreams, and fantasies; or it can be as physical as participating in a product test, a demonstration, or any activity that helps to promote a bond between the public and the subject.

• Marketers should imagine themselves in the position of the person or people they are trying to reach and be attentive to what will be most effective or desirable from the users' perspective.

• A marketing program should not simply be a presentation of what the *marketer* wants to say in order to win awards or spice-up the new business portfolio. It should reflect the mood, sentiments, and culture of the people who make up the target market.

- Cultures and customs can vary greatly within communities, cities, and certainly internationally. A marketing experience should reflect an awareness of this. If the message is not going to impress everyone, it is still advisable to exclude or alienate the smallest possible percentage of people.

- Not everyone within a target market segment agrees about every subject. To invest time and other resources in creating a marketing program, much less a marketing experience, marketers need to learn all they can about their target segment's likes, dislikes, interests, concerns and priorities, and consider the significance of wide arrays of disagreement within the target market.

- In the digital age, it should still not be assumed that everyone has "gone digital." Some people still refuse to use an ATM card or to leave messages on voice mail; therefore it is unlikely these people will provide personal data, much less purchase merchandise or services, via the Internet.

- Product sampling should not only be a way of introducing a product to the public, but should also serve as a method of observing consumer reaction with an eye toward making any necessary changes in the product or projecting its probable success rate. The process can also result in developing new selling points or even an entire campaign.

- Making consumers aware of a product by involving them in an experience with it will be remembered. That is one reason why public opinion surveys are useful.

- Field research with people regarded as favorable to the company and product can provide valuable feedback, generate positive "word-of-mouth" publicity, and produce research information based on experiences that can then be repackaged as possible marketing experiences for presentation to the public.

- Market research provides direction, helps in setting goals and making media decisions, and is invaluable in determining what the public thinks and how it *feels* about a product, if indeed it thinks about the product at all.

- Publishing current research or using survey or study information as a marketing tool can be useful as part of a public relations effort. Conducting the research can also generate fresh ideas for future marketing experiences.

- Research developed to help create a marketing experience has the potential to become an experience itself.

- The importance of market research cannot be overstated, particularly in a market climate characterized by uncertainty.

- Research should indicate the percentage of people in the target market segment that believe whatever is new or improved is probably best and therefore worth pursuing and considering, if not purchasing or subscribing outright.

- Research data must determine what people want, are buying, and doing; what they expect, but are likely willing to accept; what they dislike; what will address, neutralize, and overcome resistance; and what media best reaches the target market.

- Conduct and manage research; identify what is unique, distinctive, or sets the subject apart from others.

- Research is imperfect, yet demographic, psychographic, and other studies can be useful in crafting a well-focused marketing program.

- Creating a marketing experience places an emphasis on building relationships, but without research the process can be by trial and error, and a very costly way of doing business.

- The marketing plan provides direction and serves an extremely important function, but only if people involved in the marketing effort read it and use it.

- The essential elements of the marketing plan are the situation analysis, objectives, strategy, tactics, time line, and budget.

- As budgets of most organizations are typically strained, review the plan with an eye toward which items will benefit various departments or divisions other than marketing, and attempt to have those departments both become involved and contribute the plan's funding.

- The marketing experience should provide a reason for the public to want to respond, participate, and be a part of the process, such as an offer of a prize, gift, sample, or other incentive—especially the reward of personal recognition. Depending on the demographics of the target market, the experience can be fun, educational, or both.

- Even the most gifted marketers can't know everything about everything. A public relations professional or firm, an ad agency, or a clever in-house marketing manager should be able to develop a list of creative execution possibilities, but outside experts can make a great contribution and should be brought in to consult if that's what is required.

- Creating a plan for a marketing experience is a major undertaking that should include sales and marketing professionals as well as technical, research, legal, and others who can contribute something to the effort.

- Attracting the public by creating a physical and emotional connection to a subject was once the province of creative directors; now, to a large extent, it is partly everyone's job.

- People of certain demographic groups are thought to be generally smarter, more aware, or sophisticated. This is the same group that is perhaps also more skeptical of many overused advertising techniques and claims.

- The climate created by unusual or well-publicized radical methods of creating awareness and attracting business encourages some marketers to take risks in reaching an increasingly jaded public.

- Creating a marketing experience that resonates cannot be a hit-and-run matter. Much of the public continues to require that something be not just good, but also *fresh* and *sustaining*.

- The possibilities allow for one campaign to continue as another is tested or rolled out, as long as a cohesive message is maintained so the public will not be confused by competing campaigns.

- It is possible for a campaign to include both a single marketing experience event and an interactive experience. An ongoing program sustains loyalty and builds equity while keeping the public and the subject together.

- A plan should reach the target market on an emotional, psychological, or sensory level *and* make certain to include a "value statement" in the marketing message.

- Involve participants on as many levels as possible. Being exclusionary can work against a marketer at different times. Someone entering a program at one level might move up to another if he or she has a good opinion of the subject.

- Marketing experiences do not occur in a vacuum, but take place in the real world against an economic, political, social, and cultural backdrop that sometimes dramatically alters the environment and the mood of the moment and the market.

- Familiarity makes people comfortable. The challenge of engaging the public and the chances of succeeding are greater when a connection is created within a familiar context.

- An ongoing marketing experience—as opposed to a one-time big idea—can help build brand equity, loyalty, and a strong marketing position.

- Generate awareness and interest for a subject, even though much of the public believes there is already too much advertising and hype, and resents getting more junk mail, ads, Internet pop-ups, and spam. *How* to work against these objections is clearly a creative challenge, but despite the noise and the clutter it claims to hate, the public still responds to presentations that are entertaining, provide information, appear to be addressing needs or desires to which they can relate, and offer or promise something of value.

- Because everyone is selling doesn't guarantee that everyone is always in a mood to buy. Repeating the message as often as the budget allows and offering choices and value increase the likelihood of succeeding.

- A marketing experience can be made available for a limited time, but limiting the options *too much* work against the public interests.

- Different people are moved by different motivating factors at different times.

- Creating a marketing experience requires both the marketer and the market be receptive to the message and its presentation, promise, and timing.

- Connect with the public on its terms, especially making creative attempts to address and offer something of value to people who dislike advertising.

- The type of experience should be appropriate to both the subject and the target market. Funny promotions are generally not a good idea for health care providers and many "fun" promotions by banks fall flat as the public equates banks and money with bankers being intelligent and serious.

- An entertaining place makes people feel good and brings them back to shop and share the experience again. However the experience is designed, be welcoming, grateful, and useful.

- Do something. Offer something. Entertain. Inform. Present something that the public both wants and in which it has an interest.

- Connect with the public, engage people, hold their interest, and close the deal with planning and actions.

- Take the market's pulse to determine public tastes, needs, concerns, tolerance levels, and hot buttons.

- Many marketing experiences are initiated by life, originating with news and events triggered or driven by all segments of society.

- Factors that influence and define the experience to be created include the objective of the effort; the market to be addressed; the product, organization, subject, or industry; traditions, location, timing, and resources available to support the program.

- Know what matters most to the people and allow the strategy and tactics to reflect what the public feels is known, acceptable, and comfortable.
- Stretch creatively and don't hold back.
- Give people what they *think* they want—*and* offer them a choice of something new and different.
- Prepare well, trust your judgment, and feel good about what you are doing.

The twenty-first century arrived with some new rules. Creativity and innovation are back in style. Don't accept that an idea can't be tried because it's never been tried before. But having new opportunities to stretch and achieve exciting new things does not mean whatever worked and might still be working must be discarded because it's not *new*. Whether the process is called relationship marketing, target marketing, or whatever comes in with the new season, quality, value, ethics, creativity, and good taste have served organizations well and should continue to do so. People expect more. Great expectations provide companies with an opportunity to shine, reach out, engage, connect with the market, and create a marketing experience that brings those on both sides of the deal what they want and need.

SOURCES and REFERENCES

American Girl web site: www.americangirl.com.

Associated Press: "Boomers More Active in Some Online Tasks Than Younger People" by Anick Jesdanun, November 13, 2002.

Bubba Gump Shrimp Company Restaurant and Market. Corporate press material, 2004.

Business Intelligence by Kirk W.M. Tyson. Lombard, IL: Leading Edge Publications, 1986.

Country Music Hall of Fame and Museum web site: www .countrymusichalloffame.com.

Creating Customer Evangelists by Ben McConnell and Jackie Huba. Chicago: Dearborn Trade Publishing, 2003.

End of Marketing As We Know It, The by Sergio Zyman. New York: HarperCollins, 1999.

Experiential Marketing by Bernd H. Schmitt. New York: The Free Press, 1999.

Folio: "eXPERIENCE MARKETING" by Jane E. Zarem, October 1, 2000.

Forbes: "Thoughts on the Business of Life," May 26, 2003.

Hoovers Online Report: "Krispy Kreme Doughnuts," June 20 2004.

Interactive Excellence: Defining and Developing New Standards for the Twenty-first Century by Edwin Schloss-berg. New York: The Library of Contemporary Thought, the Ballantine Publishing Group, 1998.

John F. Kennedy Library and Museum web site: www .jfklibrary.org.

Marketing by Robert D. Hisrich. New York: Barron's, 1990.

Marketing Corporate Image by James R. Gregory with Jack G. Wiechmann. New York: McGraw-Hill/Contemporary Books; (2nd edition), 1999.

Marketing Revolution, The by Kevin J. Clancy and Robert S. Shulman. New York: HarperBusiness, 1991.

Marketing Without Advertising by Michael Phillips and Salli Rasberry. Berkley, CA: Nolo Press, 1986.

Massachusetts Daily Collegian: "Celebrities Support Wide Array of Food Products" by Jessica Pelletier, April 10, 2003.

Newsweek: "Hot Bytes, by the Dozen" by Catherine Skipp, April 28, 2003; "Dolls—They're History" by Karen Springen, December 8, 2003.

New York Times: "Touring the Future, Virtually" by Michael Marriott, March 4, 2004.

New York Times Magazine: "Girls and Dolls" by Leah Eskin, July 20, 2003. "A Thirst Quenching New York Tradition Is Being Revived" by Margaret Chiffriller, March 5, 2003.

Other Guy Blinked, The—How Pepsi Won the Cola Wars by Roger Enrico and Jesse Kornbluth. New York: Bantam Books, 1986.

PRISM Online: "Putting the Fun Back into Fundamentals" by Missy Cummings, March 2000. Published by ASEE (The American Society for Engineering Education).

Rheingold Brewing Company web site: www.rheingoldbeer.com.

Sales and Marketing Excellence: "Design Backwards" by David W. Richardson, November 2003.

Starbucks web site: ww.starbucks.com.

Steamboat Pilot (www.steamboatpilot.com): "Students pile into VW Beetle; set record," 1997.

Vision: An Executive Brief: "Experiential Marketing" by Dr. Augustine Fou. Published online at Marketing Science web site (www.mktsci.com), March 21, 2003.

Wall Street Journal: "Well, Aren't You Special" by Paula Szuchman, May 14, 2004.

INDEX

About TEXERE

Texere, a progressive and authoritative voice in business publishing, brings to the global business community the expertise and insights of leading thinkers. Our books educate, enlighten, and entertain, and provide an intersection where our authors and our readers share cutting edge ideas, practices, and innovative solutions. Texere seeks to cultivate, enhance, and disseminate information that illuminates the global business landscape.

www.thomson.com/learning/texere

About the typeface

This book was set in 12 pt Times Roman. Times Roman is a body text, serified typeface. This typeface is known for its readability and economical use of space.

Library of Congress Cataloging-in-Publication Data

Marconi, Joe.
  Creating the marketing experience : new strategies for building relationships with your target market / by Joe Marconi.
      p. cm.
  Includes bibliographical references and index.
  ISBN 0-324-20544-9 (alk. paper)
  1. Relationship marketing. 2. Target marketing. I. Title.
  HF5415.55.M335 2005
  658.8′12—dc22

2005015327